History of Japan

A Captivating Guide to Japanese History, Including Events Such as the Genpei War, Mongol Invasions, Battle of Tsushima, and Atomic Bombings of Hiroshima and Nagasaki

Free Bonus from Captivating History (Available for a Limited time)

Hi History Lovers!

Now you have a chance to join our exclusive history list so you can get your first history ebook for free as well as discounts and a potential to get more history books for free! Simply visit the link below to join.

Captivatinghistory.com/ebook

Also, make sure to follow us on Facebook, Twitter and Youtube by searching for Captivating History.

Contents

Introduction

They came from all walks of life, social classes, and religions, but they were united by their unquenchable thirst for freedom. Armed with unwavering courage, they came from southeast Asia, through China and over land bridges, into a new land. As with all primitive cultures, the first Japanese were divided into clans, clinging together for security, and built homesteads. They weren't alone. Already there was a collection of indigenous people, whose exact origin is unknown. Once the glacial waters receded, creating the Sea of Japan, the nascent country was alone and separated from China and the rest of Asia. In the first century, Japan developed independently from mainland China, but there were Chinese immigrations later on.

Japan is one of the most adaptable countries in the world. It is capable of very rapid change, even after crises that would halt the progress of other nations. When the shogunates collapsed in the 17th century, the feudal system disintegrated. Within time, though, railroads replaced ox carts. During World War I, a first-rate economy sprung up on deserted farmlands. During World War II, the modest islands of Japan burgeoned into an empire with one of the most powerful navies in the world. After the devastation of that world war, Japan emerged as one of the most modern countries in the world. The Japanese have survived frequent earthquakes and tsunamis and rebuilt their cities using enviable technologies.

The Japanese progressed throughout the eras because of the emperor, but they also progressed despite him. These are people who never let go of their sacred history, and their story is told and retold in art, film, literature, and even graphic novels across the entire world. Terms such as shoguns, samurai, haiku, anime, and manga are familiar to many in the Western world today. Westerners also learn flower arranging, martial arts, meditation, and enjoy a variety of visual and digital art forms because of the unique culture of Japan.

Chapter 1 – Children of the Sun

They trudged over to some of the 4,000 islands across Asian land bridges that floated on the seas toward the end of the glacial age. The archipelago that is Japan has only four sizable islands—Hokkaido in the north, Honshu (formerly called "Yamato") in the central region, and to the south, Shikoku and Kyushu. The northern wind is cold and dry, originating from the Asian mainland. Artifacts from the Paleolithic era some 20,000 years ago are similar to those found in Manchuria and Mongolia. The southern wind brings the typhoons, as they are conditioned by the Japan Current, or the Kuroshio, that comes from the tropics and the Oyashio Current, which is a cold current from Siberia that sweeps southward. Those that came to Japan found a hilly, mountainous country with five hundred volcanoes, though only about one hundred are currently active, the most famous of which is Mount Fuji, which dominates many Japanese paintings.

The Ainu people of Japan mostly settled in Hokkaido, as the rest of the archipelago was underwater during the glacial melting. Their appearance was proto-Caucasian or Mongoloid, and the males had full beards. Some of the Ainu people even had blue eyes. According to Japanese legend, "They lived in this place a hundred thousand years before the Children of the Sun came." The term "children of the sun" refers to the people of the Yayoi period in the third century

BCE. That corresponds with the Chinese dynastic chronicle, the *History of the Wei Kingdom*, compiled in the year 300 CE. When Japan became more populous, the Ainu were discriminated against, as they were very different in their appearance and cultural practices. Today, there are about 25,000 of them left, but most are of mixed race due to intermarriages over the years.

The Jomon period spanned from around 14,000 to 1000 BCE. Some archeologists indicate that the Ainu people were the remnants of the Jomon civilization, though others indicate they preceded the Jomon period. It is possible that the Ainu originated from the northern steppes, while the Jomon came in from the South Pacific. The Jomon people were animists who worshiped nature, not out of fear but out of respect. That was because their survival depended upon the earth. They were shorter in stature and darker than the Ainu up north. The Jomon gathered nuts and roots, and they hunted and consumed shellfish. They lived in small settlements of round thatched homes sunken two feet into the ground. A fire crackled in the middle of their dwellings, and smoke billowed out a circular opening in the roofs. These people are known for "cord pottery," which was bulbous in form and impressed with cords that formed designs. Some clay pots were half-buried and were used for storage or cooking, while others used them for religious purposes.

The Yayoi period came next and is said to date from 1000 BCE to 300 CE. The people who came during that time most likely immigrated from China. They brought with them the knowledge of the irrigated rice paddy and lived in tight-knit units with distinctive leaders. While some homes were at ground level, most were elevated above the wet fields. They used bronze decorations and weapons, including spears, swords, mirrors, and bells. In central Honshu, huge bells were found, but they were without clappers, so they were most likely hit from the outside as part of a ceremony. Such bells weren't found south of there.

The Kofun period lasted from about 300 to 538 CE. These people were more aristocratic and more militant in nature. They had swords, helmets, and shields, as well as armor and horses. Some archeologists speculate that this wave of immigration came from Korea. The dead were treated with more sophistication than in earlier periods, where bodies were buried without coffins in the fetal position. The Kofun people interred their dead in huge earthenware jars and placed mounds above the graves. Later on, they dug stone tombs. Their leaders were called emperors, a term that was taken from China once they became acquainted with each other, which was retroactively applied to previous rulers. This position was hereditary, and the emperor was considered to be of divine origins. They used their powers of persuasion to unite the many clans under their purvey, and they also used their military might.

Society during this time was divided into hereditary clans or family groupings called *uji*. The *uji* of the more powerful clans were known as *omi* to distinguish themselves from the aristocrats who were more distantly related to royalty. Certain clans held a great deal of power in Japan, and it would be similar to the aristocratic families in Western cultures, who may not have been royalty but still wielded a lot of influence over the court and its decisions. In the future, the clans in Japan would have more power than even the emperor himself.

Asuka Japan

The Kofun period was followed by the Asuka period, which ran from 538 to 710 CE. The annals of old China called Japan the "land of Wa (or "Wei)." "Wa" is a derogatory word in Chinese for "dwarf," and the Chinese considered the people of Japan inferiors to themselves.

The *uji* were separated into occupational groups. For example, some groups were in charge of ritualistic ceremonies and priestly functions, while others were tasked with matters of the state. Labor forces composed the level below, consisting mostly of skilled craftsmen, fishermen, weavers, hunters, ceramic makers, and the like. The lowest groups were the commoners and slaves.

The commoners, as expected, were poor and uneducated and farmed the land for a living. However, monks traveled to China to proselytize and brought back rice paper to Japan. Young children weren't blessed with toys, so the art of origami was developed. A child learned how to make chairs, tables, people, birds, and the like. Then they played with those creations much like a child plays with their dolls in a dollhouse.

Most people grew their own rice and raised their own vegetables, along with some for their overlords, or the princes of the provinces and towns. Slaves represented only about five percent of the population.

In terms of marriage, all children were considered legitimate regardless of whether they were born by their father's wife or a concubine. Usually, marriages were monogamous.

Mythology

In Japan, the first gods were related, being sister and brother—Izanami and Izanagi. It was believed that they dipped their sacred spear into the waters and created the islands of Japan. Amaterasu was the sun goddess and Tsukuyomi was the moon god. A bronze mirror seen among the archeological artifacts signifies the sun goddess, and a round jewel stands for the moon god. Tsukuyomi was the enemy of the emperors,

who were said to have come into being in 660 BCE, but the date is very arbitrary as the creation myths underwent continual revisions. Japanese creation stories tend to explain natural events or occurrences in noted people, like the emperors.

The first emperor of Japan, according to legend, was named Jimmu Tenno. The seat of the imperial state was Yamato (Honshu). Around 270 CE, the people from Kyushu invaded and appointed Ojin as the emperor. He was renamed Hachiman, the Shinto god of war. This deification of emperors continued all the way until 1946.

Shintoism

The Shinto religion was the first religion in Japan. The members of that sect were animists and had an array of deities. Shintoism embraced many practices, including ancestor worship, fertility rites, and a reverence for nature. The spirit, called *kami*, resided in each person and even natural objects, such as a tree or a waterfall. It was like an essence that inhabited all living things. The Shinto religion had no founder, no sacred books, no saints, and no martyrs. Shinto shrines were simple, and they still exist all over Japan. A Shinto shrine is a structure with small ascending steps and a peaked roof. Inside there are symbolic objects like bronze mirrors or swords. There are bowls placed in front for washing, as washing is a way for one to be cleansed of impurities, including spiritual ones. Shintoism was and still is the most common religion in Japan. It did not conflict with other religions but rather blended with them.

Buddhism

Buddhism was officially introduced to Japan by Korea in 552 CE, although the origins of Buddhism go much further back. It is thought that Buddhism originated in India around the first millennium BCE and then traveled to Nepal. Buddhism was personified in Siddhartha Gautama, better known as the Buddha, meaning the "Enlightened One." Gautama wasn't a deity; he was human. Throughout his life, he brooded over the human condition and found that it was associated with suffering, which would give rise to desire. In order to reach a state of true happiness and peace, which is called Nirvana, it is necessary to rid oneself of earthly desires. One has to, therefore, follow an eightfold path consisting of right understanding, thought, speech, conduct, livelihood, effort, mindfulness, and concentration. It is a religion that emphasizes ethical conduct (*sila*), mental discipline (*samadhi*), and wisdom (*panna*). There are numerous Buddhist temples in Japan, but the temple of Horyu-ji is acknowledged as being the oldest wooden structure in the world. It is also one of the most beautiful temples in all of Japan. Today, it is a complex consisting of a monastery, library, lecture halls, refectory, and a five-story pagoda. Buddhism is the second-largest religion in Japan today.

The Japanese tradition of Buddhism is known as Mahayana Buddhism, and its adherents believe in the bodhisattvas, who are spiritual beings who have postponed their own state of eternal bliss in order to help humans along the path of salvation. At the end of time, they believe that a bodhisattva, named Miroku or Maitreya Buddha, will come to save humanity and bring it into a state of purity and paradise. This Buddha mirrors the Christ figure as taught in traditional Christianity.

The Soga vs. Nakatomi Clans

The *uji* in Yamato separated over the issue of adopting Buddhism or Shintoism. The Soga clan preferred to make the national religion Buddhism, while the Nakatomi clan preferred Shintoism. The debate started in 552 CE when the Japanese ally of Korea, Paekche, sent an image of Buddha to the imperial court. When an epidemic struck, Emperor Kinmei ordered the Buddhist images to be destroyed along with the Hoko-ji temple, also called the Asuka-dera temple.

In 585, another pestilence struck, and Emperor Yomei found out that some Korean priests had two images of the Buddha, and those were thrown into a moat. When the pestilence persisted, the emperor ordered the images to be restored, after which the plague then ceased. Korean priests and nuns arrived soon after, and Buddhism began to thrive. Empress Suiko, who reigned from 592 to 628 CE and who was a devoted Buddhist, had a nephew, Prince Shotoku, who was a scholar and politician. Prince Shotoku was the son of Emperor Yomei, and he lived from 574 to 622 CE and wrote a commentary on Buddhism called *Śrīmālādevī Siṃhanāda Sūtra*. A sutra is an aphorism or maxim based on a recognized truth. The term is also used in Muslim and Hindi teachings.

Confucianism

Confucius was a Chinese scholar who developed a practical code for right understanding, the second principle of the eightfold Buddhist path. Some people perceive of Confucianism as a religion, but it is more so a system of right thinking. It was from the studies of Confucius that Prince Shotoku created the first constitution of Japan in 604 CE. The Twelve Level Cap and Rank System of civil service was installed, and that was a major change for Japan. In this system, rank was based on merit and achievement instead of hereditary alone. This system inspired other cap and rank systems later on.

Relations with China

Prince Shotoku, who was an important politician during the reign of Empress Suiko, felt it was essential for Japan to establish good relations with China, so he sent fourteen missions to China. His faux-pas occurred prior to the first mission when he sent a letter to China. In this letter, he addressed China as the land of the setting sun while calling Japan the land of the rising sun. Chinese Emperor Yang of Sui took this as a deprecation, as he was accustomed to foreigners portraying themselves as subservient to China. However, the Buddhist monks and well-versed statesmen of Japan were able to overcome that drawback, so the two countries were able to share the knowledge and technology of the time. What's more, a paradigm had now been created for the maintenance of peace and understanding with China and other East Asian countries. Of course, throughout the years, hostilities occasionally arose that had found their footing in the politics and trade policies of other nations.

The Fujiwara (Nakatomi) Clan

One of the major clans in Yamato was the Fujiwara. The term "Fujiwara" was the revised name for the Nakatomi clan, and they particularly opposed the Soga clan because of its wholehearted support of Buddhism. In the year 645, they staged a coup, which then gave rise to a new imperial line. The first emperor of that line was Emperor Tenchi (or Tenji), and he seized power in 645 CE.

Tenchi applied many reforms, called the Taika Reforms, to the hierarchical structure, and he reestablished heredity as the foundation of imperial lineage; however, merit was also honored and expected of the emperors and royal families. Buddhism was made the national religion, although Shintoism was tolerated. Imperial power was fortified, and the bureaucracy was sophisticated under Tenchi's rule.

The Taiko Reforms and the Taiho Code

In the year 645, the central government made many widespread changes that were based on Chinese systems. The central administration was subdivided hierarchically and abolished private land ownership. The land was nationalized in the name of the emperor and parceled out to able-bodied men. Taxes were charged on grain, rice, and other crops. The lower-levels who couldn't afford such taxes were given lots of land, which up to five families would till.

Under the Taiho Code of 702, the old tax-exempt status of the elite classes was eliminated, but the tax reform was very gradual in order to prevent rebellions. There were taxes on crops, crafts, and textiles. Military service was required, but more tax payments could be substituted for that. Despite the fact that the changes were gradually introduced, the taxes incurred by farmers were very burdensome and produced hardships. Taxes were usually paid in the form of rice or another crop and occasionally copper.

Nara Japan 710 – 794 CE

During this period, the capital was moved to Heijo, also known as Nara, located in south-central Honshu. As the Japanese learned more from the Chinese model of rule, they designed their new capital to resemble Chang'an (modern-day Xi'an), a city that ruled as a capital for many dynasties in China.

Politics in Nara were designed around court life. During this period, the emperors became progressively weaker. Interclan rivalries usually resulted in one clan or the other gaining dominance over the political scene, but the Fujiwara maintained most of the control, although it ebbed and flowed at times.

The nobility was absorbed with the maintenance of ritual ceremonies. They performed beautiful music and dance performances, some of which were imported from China. These performances were extremely elaborate, containing grandiose costumes and fanciful masks.

The Taiho Code of 702 was upgraded to the Yoro Code of 718. The Yoro Code was a revision of the basic code regarding governmental administration, but it also added on a penal code, a department of religion, and a declaration asserting the divinity of the emperor. Those departments managed the religious rites of the country and determined the penalties for crimes.

Local governments consisted of provinces, districts, and villages. Those who held higher offices were allotted larger tracts of land. As a result, there came to be landowners who owned huge plots of land. Many aristocrats and monastic orders were tax-exempt, and although they did reclaim unused land for agrarian purposes, it was labeled as state property and likewise wasn't taxable. These tax-exempt lands caused hardships for the rest of the population and placed even more of a burden upon the ordinary cultivators than it did during the Asuka era of the 6th century. This stimulated agrarian poverty and created a whole segment of vagrants, who were called *ronin*, although that term later evolved to mean something else.

During the period of Nara Japan, there was a series of natural disasters, in addition to a smallpox epidemic which, combined with the disasters, killed a quarter of the people. The emperor at the time, Shomu, blamed himself and felt that his lack of religiosity caused these calamities. He made up for it by constructing the Buddhist temple of Todai-ji. That shrine houses the world's largest bronze statue of the Buddha.

Chapter 2 – Warring Clans

Heian Japan 794 – 1185 CE

Again, the capital of Japan was moved—this time to Heian-kyo, or current-day Kyoto in south-central Japan. The main government of Heian times was obsessed with ritualistic observances. Costumes became even more elaborate, and there were even fastidious regulations regarding the colors of the robes the royal family was supposed to wear.

Throughout the Asuka period to the Heian era, tax-exempt property was increasing. The peasants could no longer shoulder the burden, so the administrators worked out a new system that resembled feudal times. Under this, the peasants were permitted to transfer their lands to a landowner in exchange for being placed under the owner's tax-free status, and with this, they also received protection against robbers and other criminals. This was done as a sheer matter of economic and physical survival.

From the 7th century to the 10th century, hostilities sometimes arose in the northern area of Japan, specifically in Mutsu Province where the Emishi tribes had settled. Ethnologists argue about their relationship with the indigenous people of Japan, known as the Ainu. Ethnologists have proposed that they are one and the same and date back to prehistoric times. However, those people had different racial characteristics than the tribes who came into Japan from Asia. For instance, Emishi males grew full beards and had skin tones that differed from that of the Japanese population. The Emishi were also among the most skilled horsemen in the Eastern world. Many of the Emishi people rejected the power of the emperor and resisted the pseudo-feudal structures that were emerging. After repeated conflicts, many of them fled northward and settled in Honshu, the largest island of Japan.

Other people on the islands of Japan followed the dictates of the emperor, who was the supreme head of the country. When he became older, he retired but maintained an impressive amount of power if he so wished. The emperors were often called "cloistered emperors," as they usually went to monasteries to retire.

As feudalism became more structured during the 12th century, the landowners and lords appointed warriors to guard their land tracts. The chiefs of these tracts were called "Commanders-in-Chief of the Expeditionary Force against the Barbarians," or *Sei-i Tashogun*. However, it is the shortened form of that name that has made its way into the collective conscious today—shogun. Their secondary warlords were known as *daimyo*, and they wielded power over the military function of the estates. Their warriors were called *bushi* but are commonly known as samurai to Westerners. *Ronin*, the term discussed above that means vagrants, also came to mean those samurai who had no lord. There were a plethora of reasons for why they had no master, for example, the death of his master, the loss of his master's favor, or the loss of his master's status. Some faithful samurai chose to commit ritual suicide, known as seppuku, as a sign of their ultimate loyalty to their master. Others wandered the country in search of new *daimyo* to follow. Usually, shogun and *daimyo* who hired *ronin* were considered to be less powerful.

While the general assumption was that the *ronin* were honorable men, this wasn't always the case. Because a samurai with no master had virtually no duties to perform and no other employable skills, he often became a criminal. Other ronin organized rebellions in order to carve out some territory of their own.

The population on these protected tracts were the peasants, who were divided into farmers, craftsmen, and merchants. Although the farmers were the poorest and dressed only in hemp, artisans or craftsmen were below them, and merchants were considered to be one of the two lowest classes. They were rated in a lower class because it was assumed they had a lower moral standing because of the greed, avarice, and dishonesty they often manifested. In time, merchants became very powerful because of their wealth.

The *burakumin*, on the other hand, was an outcast group at the bottom of the Japanese social order. These were people considered to be impure and were relegated to begging. The more enterprising among them became entertainers, such as musicians, dancers, or street performers. Others were hired as executioners or undertakers, as these occupations were considered to be tainted since they dealt with dead bodies. The *burakumin* actually lived in their own communities called *buraku*, and the status of being a part of this community was hereditary.

The Samurai

A samurai was a highly trained warrior who was a part of the military nobility. He lived according to Bushido, a set of precepts that dictated how to fight with honor, obedience, and dignity. The samurai was sworn to fealty to the shogun, the *daimyo*, and, ultimately, the emperor. A samurai warrior pledged his life to those authorities, and like the knights of the later medieval ages in Europe, they always strived to adhere to chivalrous conduct.

Eight virtues were specified in Bushido:

Righteousness – This meant justice and the support for their actions.

Courage – This was greater than a display of bravery. It was almost like blind obedience to a belief.

Courtesy – This wasn't superficial politeness. It meant a sense of genuine empathy and respect for the feelings of others.

Benevolence – This meant having mercy and sympathy for those who were in need.

Honesty – This meant forthrightness on all of their dealings.

Honor – A samurai was expected to do what was required but never to relish destruction or killing for its own sake.

Loyalty – Faithfulness to the *daimyo* and the shogun was expected, regardless of payment or reward.

Character – Every samurai was expected to manifest moral conduct in all aspects of his life, without exception.

The samurai learned Bushido from a very young age. Initially, they were taught the military arts from their fathers or other adult male members of the family. Then they were transferred to the mentorship of a fencing instructor and others with specific talents. They learned meditation and the martial arts, usually jujutsu. Each samurai warrior pledged his entire life to the defense of the leader of the province, even unto death. The ultimate purpose of such a strict code, of course, was the preservation of the shogun as the autocratic leader.

Clan Warfare

Basically, the Heian period was characterized by internecine warfare among the prominent clans—the Fujiwara, the Tairo, and the Minamoto. The Emishi people were always considered to be enemies by all of the clans. The best description of this period was the warrior era.

During Heian times, the central government progressively lost power because the nobles and the head of the clans seized more tax-free land, thus depriving the government of needed taxes to support the country. As the central government declined, so did the number of imperial military forces needed for defense. To compensate for that, each of the castles belonging to the clan leaders employed more and more samurai. There were three wars that were fought over control of the land and its people during that time—the Zenkunen War, or the Early Nine Years' War (1051 to 1063), the Gosannen War, or the Later Three-Year War (1083 to 1089), and the Genpei War (1180 to 1185).

The Zenkunen War took place in Mutsu Province on Honshu and was fought between the imperial army and the Abe clan, one of the oldest in all of Japan and a throwback to the former Yamato clan. This war was triggered by the Abe clan's harsh tax policy, as they ignored the wishes of the governor, the one who should have been overseeing the region and levying taxes. With the assistance of the Minamoto and Kiyowara clans, Emperor Nijo maintained control, and the Abe clan lost the war and was forced to alter its tax policy.

The Gosannen War was waged among three families from the Kiyohara clan: Masahira, Iehira, and Narihira. The governor of Mutsu Province attempted to negotiate with the families but to no avail. So, Governor Minamoto no Yoshiie was forced to use his own forces to stop the fighting, along with the help of the Fujiwara clan. As a result, there was severe devastation of the farmlands in Mutsu Province, followed by food shortages.

The Genpei War

During the late Heian era, clan rivalries were at its peak as each grappled for power, namely the Taira and Minamoto clans. In 1160, a war-mongering general by the name of Taira no Kiyomori of the Taira clan ruled Kyoto and had set up an entirely samurai-led government of his own making. Kiyomori wanted to expand his domains, so he placed his two-year-old grandson, Antoku, on the throne after the abdication of Emperor Takakura and moved the imperial throne from Kyoto to Fukuhara-kyo. In doing so, he was able to keep the royal family under his control. Kiyomori had a reputation for being a tyrant, and he was absolutely ruthless. Even many of the samurai under him had misgivings about him.

In the year 1180, the conflict came to a head. Former emperor Go-Shirakawa's son, Mochihito, felt as if he had been denied his rightful place on the throne and supported the other powerful clan of the time, the Minamoto clan. Minamoto no Yorimasa, a warrior and a poet, along with Mochihito, sent out for a call to arms, which Kiyomori did not appreciate. He called for the arrest of Mochihito, who took refuge in a Buddhist monastery. Many monks at those times were warrior monks; however, they did not prove to be strong enough to protect Yorimasa and Mochihito. So, they abandoned the monastery and took flight until they reached the River Uji. The bloody battle continued there, but the Minamoto forces were no match for the Taira, despite the fact that they had dismantled the wooden bridge over the river. Prince Mochihito initially was able to escape, but soon after, he was captured and killed. Minamoto no Yorimasa committed seppuku, ending the battle.

General Yoritomo of the Minamoto clan took over the leadership of the clan and persuaded more clans to ally themselves with him, the most influential being the Takeda clan. While Yoritomo and his men attacked from the front, the Takeda clan and others friendly to the Minamoto cause attacked from behind. This strategy worked, and the Minamoto clan finally managed to get the upper hand.

In September of 1180, the Battle of Ishibashiyama occurred. It was a surprise night attack against the Minamoto, who were joined by some of the disillusioned forces of the Taira forces, hoping to disrupt the enormous army of the Taira, which numbered close to 3,000. But their efforts failed, as the Minamoto only had around 300 men, and so, the overwhelming Taira army still won.

The fighting continued into the next year, but soon it would cease. In the spring of 1181, Taira no Kiyomori died, and around that same time, Japan was struck by famine. The Taira tried to attack a cousin of Yoritomo, Minamoto no Yoshinaka, but they were unsuccessful. This was the last course of action in the Genpei War for nearly two years.

At the Battle of Kurikara in June of 1183, the tide finally swung into the favor of the Minamoto clan. Minamoto no Yoshinaka and Minamoto no Yukiie cleverly set up their mountain forces in such a way that their numbers looked immense. Because the bulk of the Minamoto force appeared to be a desirable target, the Taira came raging up the mountain to attack. During the course of their ascent, two hidden divisions of the Minamoto army attacked the Taira army in the center and in the rear. The strategy was extremely successful, and it turned the war into the Minamoto clan's favor.

The Minamoto were having internecine disputes of their own that continued throughout this period. Minamoto no Yoshinaka, who was a strong commander at the Battle of Kurikara, was feuding with his cousins, Yoritomo and Yoshitsune, for control of the Minamoto clan. Yoshinaka and Yukiie conspired to set up a new imperial court in the north, away from the influence of the Taira clan, but before that could happen, Yukiie told their plans to Emperor Go-Shirakawa. As a result, the betrayed Yoshinaka took control of Kyoto. In the early years of 1184, Yoshinaka burned the Buddhist temple that the emperor was hiding in, taking him into custody. Yoshitsune soon arrived, along with his brother Noriyori and a considerable force, and at the River Uji, where an earlier battle had taken place, the cousins fought each other. Yoshinaka was defeated and killed.

While that was occurring, the Taira clan had gained custody of Kiyomori's infant grandson, Antoku, who still officially held the throne. He was accompanied by his grandmother, and they traveled with the Taira forces.

In 1185, on the southern coast of Honshu, the Minamoto tricked the Taira army into thinking the next engagement was going to be a land battle. The subterfuge was accomplished by having their scouts light many bonfires on the shore. However, the Minamoto were geared up toward a sea battle. As the Taira ships drew close to the shores of Honshu in the Straits of Shimonoseki, between the islands of Honshu and Kyushu, the Minamoto attacked them. Initially, the battle favored the Taira, but the tide changed, and the Minamoto ultimately ended up prevailing. Most of the Minamoto clan's success was due to a general named Taguchi defecting from the Taira side in the middle of the heavy action, as it was a vicious battle with a great deal of hand-to-hand combat on the decks of ships. The six-year-old Emperor Antoku and his grandmother perished, along with many of the Taira nobles. This battle, the Battle of Dan-no-ura, was a humiliating defeat for the Taira clan, and with this defeat, the Genpei War was all but won, paving the way for the establishment of the Kamakura shogunate in 1185.

The Emaki Scrolls

Japanese history was recorded on silk handscrolls called *emaki*, and they are held either horizontally or vertically. Some narrate the stories about the Zenkunen War or the Gosannen War, while others tell tales about notable figures. One of the most notable of the scrolls told the story about Sugawara no Michizane, a scholar who was engrossed with the studies of the Chinese classics. He was appointed to the governor of Sanuki Province, and during his time in this position, Michizane stepped in to help with the Ako Incident. This incident was between Emperor Uda, who reigned between the years of 887 to 897, and Fujiwara no Mototsune over Mototsune's role in the court after Emperor Uda gained the throne. Michizane assisted Emperor Uda in the affair, helping him regain power from the Fujiwara clan. Emperor Uda gave key positions in the court to those who were not from the Fujiwara clan, including Michizane. However, when Uda abdicated the throne, Michizane was surrounded by enemies from the Fujiwara. As a result, Fujiwara no Tokihira helped to demote Michizane, who died in exile. After his death, many disasters occurred in Japan, including famine and plague. The superstitious people then deified him and erected a Shinto shrine in his name called the Kitano Tenman-gu. The handscroll depicting Michizane's downfall is still in existence and is displayed at the Watanabe Museum in Tottori, Japan.

One of the most quoted poets of the Heian period was Ki no Tsurayuki. His poems were also recorded and illustrated on the *emaki.* His poems were semi-religious and reverent, and they were very popular in their day. They encapsulated facets of nature, romance, or a deeply emotional human experience. One such poem demonstrates the depth of the human experience:

A dewdrop

It is not, my heart, on a flower

Fallen; yet

With a breath of wind

My concern grows deeper.

Women poets were equally respected and carried the same themes, such as this by Nakatsukasa: "Those cherry blossoms that I keep coming to see year after year, O mist do not rise now and hide them."

Kamakura Japan 1185 – 1333

The feudal system became more complex during the Kamakura period. Instead of merely the *daimyo*, there arose the constables or military governors who were called *shugo*, who served a judicial function, and the stewards of the land who were called *jito*. Emperors became less powerful during this period of time, as did their royal families. The shogun was essentially now the head of the central policy-making body, and a military-like structure permeated governmental bodies.

In 1192, the first shogun of the Kamakura period, Minamoto no Yoritomo, had his father-in-law, Hojo no Tokimasa from the Hojo clan, who had assisted in the Minamoto clan's win at the Battle of Dan-no-ura, as his advisor. Ironically enough, the Hojo clan was descended from the Taira, but they did not fight alongside their ancestors. Tokimasa's daughter, Masako, became the regent of their infant son, Yoriie, after Yoritomo died in 1199, which gave the Hojo clan great power.

The heart of this shogunate was in Kamakura, which is a picturesque seaside town outside of today's Tokyo. The actual capital of Japan at the time was Kyoto, however, and this was where the administrative functions were performed.

In 1266, Kublai Khan, the renowned leader of the Mongols, mandated that Japan become a vassal to their great empire. He sent emissaries to Japan with that command, but the Chinzei Bugyo, or the Defense Commissioner for the West, sent them away, and eventually, the Mongols sailed to Japan in order to start a war. The Japanese samurai won some decisive battles against the great khan, but a typhoon interfered with their conflict. The Mongols withdrew, but Kublai Khan swore he would return.

After the Mongolian withdrawal, the Kamakura military worked steadily and built an impressive sea wall surrounding Hakata Bay along present-day Fukuoka, on the island of Kyushu. In 1281, Kublai Khan did return. However, the great sea wall built by the Kamakura laborers confined the fighting to the narrow beach. The Battle of Koan, also known as the Second Battle of Hakata Bay, raged for 53 days, but a typhoon again interfered. Swollen streams flowed in from the sea, and thousands of Chinese and Mongolian sailors and soldiers and their mercenary Korean troops were sucked up by the drenched sand and sunk down into the depths of the sea. The khan never returned. This Kyushu port was very accessible to foreign invaders, but because of the sea wall, Japan was able to keep enemies at bay until 1945!

Arts and Religion

Although literature wasn't prominent during the Kamakura era, there were some artifacts and scrolls from that period. The scrolls were similar to the *emaki* of Heian Japan, but true likenesses of prominent individuals were adopted. Scrolls with those portraits were called *nise-e*. One such scroll, the "Hungry Ghosts," depicts the lessons of Buddhism about the levels of hell. These were moral sayings like, "The difference between passion and addiction is between a divine spark and a flame that incinerates," and "If the dreams I have on every blackberry-colored night were real, I would reveal my feelings to him."

Buddhism continued its dominance in the Kamakura age. Four branches of Buddhism emerged. The Pure Land sect indicated that fervent devotion to the Amida Buddha was sufficient enough to ensure salvation. The Jodo sect emphasized faith to bring about salvation, and the Nichiren sect stressed the chant "Hail to the Sutra of the Lotus of the Wonderful Law." The fourth sect, and one which is still very popular today, is Zen Buddhism. More effort is required of the followers of Zen Buddhism than the others, as they, for instance, emphasize the stages of disciplined concentration during meditation.

The fall of the Kamakura regime is characterized by the factor that accounts for the downfalls of many regimes—power struggles and factionalism among rival parties. The most common impetus for the domination of one regime over another is wealth. And as the elites and members of the royal families vie for larger portions of the wealth, societies can become corrupt and eventually are absorbed by their own indulgence. As the rise of the shoguns and the power of the *shugo* and the *jito* increased, imperial power decreased.

Chapter 3 – The Two Imperial Courts

Due to the turmoil incurred toward the end of the Kamakura period, resentment of the Hojo clan, which was the power behind the administration in Japan, rose.

In 1331, Emperor Go-Daigo conspired to overthrow the Kamakura shogunate, as it had made militarism so predominant in the country. He ended the practice of having cloistered emperors and clamored for control. Go-Daigo rallied some officials and members of the court to come to his support, and then he raised an army. This triggered the Genko War, which ran until 1333. Initially, Go-Daigo enjoyed some success, but the forces of the Kamakura shogunate came together, and Go-Daigo was forced to flee to a monastery at Kasagi. The Hojo clan themselves raided the temple, but Go-Daigo escaped. The Kakamura army under Ashikaga Takauji was then sent after him, but he changed loyalties and supported Go-Daigo. Kyoto was then established as the city that held the imperial power, and the Kamakura shogunate was dismantled.

Go-Daigo continued to be in control after this war and brought about what was known as the Kenmu Restoration. However, his ally, Ashikaga Takauji, became a turncoat and appointed himself shogun.

He seized power in Kyoto and passed the imperial power to Kogon, a senior member of the imperial family. Go-Daigo himself was a junior member of that line and moved his court south to Yoshino in a mountainous area.

There were now two rival courts—Kogon in the north and Go-Daigo in the south.

Ashikaga Japan 1336 – 1573 CE

In 1392, the third Ashikaga shogun, Yoshimitsu, invited Go-Daigo back, promising to share power with him. However, Yoshimitsu never fulfilled his promise, and this period, the Ashikaga period, was characterized by political turbulence. Gradually, the factions that supported Go-Daigo faded away. The fact that the various factions traded control and power prolonged the lack of central leadership and stunted progress. The shogunate was the primary root of power in Japan, and the country was virtually a checkerboard of shogun power bases. Because of this, some historians have called this period the dark ages of Japan.

Greedy *daimyos* warred with each other and carved out larger and larger chunks of *shoen*, which were lands that were tax-free. In accumulating more of these lands, it only continued to undermine the emperor's power and contributed to the growth of the clans. In 1390, the Yamana clan owned as many as eleven provinces only to be reduced to ruling only two provinces after repeated conflicts with other clans. Such strife caused the country to resemble a piecemeal pattern of individual *daimyos*. The samurai and the people generally ignored the imperial court and followed the commands of their individual *daimyos*, leading the central power in the country to be decentralized.

Because of burdensome taxes and the dishonesty of money-lenders, the peasants revolted in 1428. This rebellion, called the Shocho uprising, had as its primary aim debt cancellation. The Ashikaga shogunate did not issue the debt cancellation, but due to the heavy looting, the peasants still achieved their goal since the proofs of their debts had been destroyed. In 1441, a peasants' rebellion, called the Kakitsu uprising, was also successful and contributed to the weakening of the Ashikaga regime. Again, its goal was debt cancellation.

Revolts weren't just reserved for the underprivileged class. Buddhist monasteries had structures akin to feudal divisions and even employed their own samurai warriors. During the 14th and 15th centuries, monks united with the peasants against the overwhelming power of the *daimyos* and shoguns. The Buddhist monks formed small leagues composed of themselves and oppressed peasants, called the *Ikko-ikki*, with *ikko* meaning single-minded. These *Ikko-ikki* groups were a frequent source of violent uprisings. The *Ikko-ikki* groups usually started out as mobs but became more sophisticated in time, wearing armor and toting weapons. They opposed samurai rule, as the shoguns and their warrior troops were responsible for most of the taxes.

The Onin War

The Onin War erupted in 1467 over the succession of the next shogun. In 1464, Ashikaga Yoshimasa, the shogun at the time, realized he had no one to succeed him as he had no heir. He convinced his brother, Ashikaga Yoshimi, to abandon the life of a monk and become his heir instead. However, Yoshimasa gave birth to a son the very next year, throwing the line of succession into question. Yoshimasa's wife, Hino Tomiko, did not want to relinquish the title of shogun to someone other than her son, and she had the backing of powerful samurai clans, namely the clan of Yamana Sozen. Yoshimi, on the other hand, had the support of a powerful clan, the Hosokawa clan.

In 1467, the war had become quite serious, as the Eastern Army of Hosokawa began to face off against the Western Army of Yamana. These armies were evenly matched, with both having about 80,000 men each. Several battles occurred, and even when Hosokawa and Yamana died in 1473, the fighting continued. While the Hosokawa clan won and was able to place Yoshimasa's son as the next shogun, there wasn't much of Kyoto left to rule. As a result of the Onin War, a huge portion of Kyoto was destroyed. After that, looting occurred until the city was nearly in ruins. With the exception of the most powerful of the *daimyos*, poverty arose even in the imperial family. In fact, Emperor Go-Nara (ruled 1526 to 1557) was forced to sell his own calligraphy in the streets of Kyoto!

Commerce and Mercantilism

While political upheavals cropped up in various provinces in Japan, the lower classes had freedoms they had never before experienced. Small and large urban centers sprung up, and trade was initiated in this isolated country. There was international trade with China and Korea. The Ming dynasty in China opened relations with Japan after the Mongols were defeated, and as a result of this mercantile expansion, Japan imported silk, books, art, and porcelain products. They exported lumber, pearls, gold, sulfur, painted folded fans, and swords.

Art and Culture

While the samurai and shoguns were engaged in warfare, the people sought some kind of relief, and they found it in the theaters and the arts.

Noh, meaning skill or talent, refers to a specific art form that began in the 14th century and incorporates masks and costumes in a dance-based performance. The actors usually wear wigs and face masks, or they paint their faces white. Themes for these performances include religious and historical events, supernatural worlds, or some mix of both. The popularity of the *noh* theater faded during the Heian period, but it was revived during the Ashikaga period. In fact, *noh* theaters still exist today.

Another important aspect of Japanese culture at this time was Zen culture, which gave impetus to an expansion of the arts. These were often tangible arts like miniature landscape gardening, Zen gardens that stressed simplicity and minimalism, the cultivation of bonsai dwarf trees, flower arranging, and tea ceremonies.

Oda Nobunaga: A Tale of the Honorable and Dishonorable

Oda Nobunaga (1534–1582) was one of the most powerful *daimyos* during this warring period of Japan. He was single-minded, ambitious, and ruthless. He once said, "If the cuckoo does not sing, I will kill it!"

Despite his cruelty, Nobunaga was the right man to reunite Japan, which had become a country of mini-kingdoms. He was determined to rid the country of the Takeda, the Saito, Mori, Uesugi, Asakura, Asai, and Hojo clans. The Hojo clan was a holdover from Kamakura Japan, and the others were clans that built up strength throughout the years. Nobunaga wasn't a paragon of Bushido virtue. When he was in the process of conquering the castle of Takeda Katsuyori during the Battle of Nagashino in 1575, he forced Katsuyori out, which went against the Bushido code of courtesy and benevolence that should have been shown toward the head of a castle. Katsuyori then fled to the residence of Oyamada, his retainer, who was likewise among the dishonorable warriors of those treacherous times. When Oyamada refused Katsuyori entry, Katsuyori committed seppuku, thus demonstrating the Bushido principles of rectitude and loyalty. Similarly, Asakura Yoshikage of the Asakura clan was forced to commit seppuku when his cousin betrayed him after Nobunaga defeated his armies and tore apart his castle.

The Buddhists weren't simply monks absorbed in daily meditation. Their sprawling estates and defense forces were a viable threat to Nobunaga's power. In the year 1571, he and his troops entered the Enryakuji temple, destroyed thousands of buildings there, and slaughtered many of the monks.

In 1574, Nobunaga placed the great fortress of Nagashima under siege. This wasn't a shogunate fortress; it was one of the many fortifications built by the *Ikko-ikki*, that is, the Buddhist warrior/peasant alliances. Nobunaga's faithful samurai, Hashiba

Hideyoshi, led the initial charges in the year 1576. He was supposed to be reinforced by Akechi Mitsuhide, another samurai who had allied himself with the *Ikko-ikki*. Hideyoshi was a samurai with an uncanny sense of battlefield strategy, and the Mori fortress, Ishiyama Hongan-ji, was taken over by Nobunaga with Hideyoshi's help. Eventually, Nobunaga was able to secure this fortress by completely cutting off the supplies for the *Ikko-ikki*, and then he set the whole building aflame. Akechi Mitsuhide never actually showed up to aid them as he had promised. Instead, he conspired against Nobunaga and wanted to eliminate him.

Hideyoshi was then dispatched to fight the Takeda clan at the Battle of Tedorigawa in 1577, successfully doing so. Nobunaga declared himself a minister and spent some time resting his weary warriors at Honno-ji, a temple in Kyoto.

In 1582, Mitsuhide attacked Nobunaga at the Honno-ji temple. He and his men separated Nobunaga from his men and cornered Nobunaga and his small group of men inside the temple. Seeing that he and his small unit were outnumbered by Mitsuhide's men, Nobunaga knew the end was near. He didn't want to be paraded in humiliation before jeering crowds, so he committed seppuku in one of the inner rooms.

Mitsuhide wasn't satisfied with the elimination of Nobunaga, however. Nobunaga's son and heir, Nobutada, was at the battle at the Ishiyama fortress when he heard about his father's death. Mitsuhide chased him and cornered Nobutada at Nijo Castle, but Nobutada committed seppuku, according to Bushido.

Mitsuhide then carried out a coup d-état over the powerful Oda clan. His treachery shocked the imperial court, who refused to back him.

Hashiba Hideyoshi, Nobunaga's samurai, rushed over to wreak revenge upon Mitsuhide and his men in the Battle of Yamazaki. Instead of confronting him out in the open fields, Mitsuhide foolishly had his men climb Mount Tennozan. It was a dangerous climb, but he thought that the higher ground would give him the advantage. He was wrong. Hashiba Hideyoshi brought archbuses with him, which were devices that could shoot multiple arrows. Thus, he pommeled Mitsuhide's warriors, and they were forced to descend the mountain and move to an open plain to continue the battle.

When Hideyoshi began to conduct a full-frontal assault on Mitsuhide and his troops, the warriors scattered in panic, including Mitsuhide himself, who lived up to his bad reputation by deserting his own troops. He met his just fate when he fled toward the town of Ogurusu and was killed by bandits. Mitsuhide only ruled as shogun for thirteen days.

Toyotomi Hideyoshi (1537–1598)

For his courage, Hashiba Hideyoshi was given the clan name Toyotomi by the elite Fujiwara clan. He named his infant son, Tsurumatsu, as heir. Hideyoshi had a different approach than his *daimyo*, Nobunaga, and revised Nobunaga's famous cuckoo-saying with this: "If the cuckoo doesn't sing, I'll make it!"

The Osaka Castle was built in 1583 by Toyotomi Hideyoshi to celebrate his ascendancy. The site was built upon the grounds of the original *Ikko-ikki* temple of Ishiyama Hongan-ji. It covered 86 acres and had numerous decorated turrets and towers.

Like Nobunaga, Hideyoshi had Japanese reunification as his goal. In 1585, he seized the small island of Shikoku from the revolutionary leader, Chosokabe Motochika. He prized that island as it had the beautiful castle of Nishinomiya on it. Winning the battle at Nishinomiya was an easy victory as Hideyoshi had 113,000 troops against Motochika's 40,000.

One of Hideyoshi's samurai generals, who was also his nephew, was Hashiba Hidetsugu. Hidetsugu was Hideyoshi's heir-apparent after the death of his own son and his half-brother. Hideyoshi relied on Hidetsugu for his martial skills. However, when Hideyoshi's next son, Hideyori, was born, Hideyoshi considered Hidetsugu to be a potential threat to his rule as the imperial regent. So, in 1593, after

Hidetsugu was accused of plotting against Hideyoshi and his family, Hideyoshi commanded Hidetsugu to commit seppuku. Obediently, Hidetsugu and some of his faithful samurai accompanied him to the top of Mount Koya, where they carried out Hideyoshi's orders. Hideyoshi was especially merciless, though, and ordered that Hidetsugu's entire family, including the children, be killed! Only two of his daughters were spared.

Hideyoshi saw threats everywhere, and his blind ambition for a dictatorial form of control made him very paranoid. He had at the Osaka Castle a master of the tea ceremony, Sen no Rikyu. Rikyu was also an accomplished poet, and he made many changes in the tea ceremony and influenced other cultural changes. Rikyu was very popular among the people, and Hideyoshi felt that this modest man was also a threat. In the year 1591, he commanded Rikyu to commit seppuku. As he was preparing the seppuku ritual, Rikyu held a tea ceremony and invited his closest friends to it. After they had finished their tea, he donated a tea bowl to each. He then took his own and smashed it against the wall, saying, "Never again shall this cup, polluted by misfortune, be used by man." He then recited a verse surrendering his soul to eternity through Buddha before killing himself.

Hideyoshi also felt threatened by the budding growth of Christianity and spoke out against it. Hideyoshi had been firmly rooted in the old traditions of feudal Japan, and he viewed any change in religion as another potential threat. As Japan was being opened up to commerce and the mercantilism of the Muromachi, or Ashikaga, period, some European missionaries came in from Spain and Portugal. Many of the mainstream Catholics fled underground during Hideyoshi's rule, but there were several noted individuals who were arrested by Hideyoshi's troops. In the year 1597, he executed 26 self-confessed Catholics by crucifying them at Nagasaki. They are called the "Twenty-Six Martyrs of Japan," and a memorial stone was placed where they shed their blood.

Another possible threat to Hideyoshi was Oda Nobunaga's younger son, Nobukatsu. One of the great samurais under Nobunaga was Tokugawa Ieyasu. Ieyasu, like Hideyoshi, had a firm belief in the reunification of Japan. Ieyasu actually outranked Hideyoshi and was his enemy, but this was only for a short period of time.

In 1584, at the Battle of Komaki and Nagakute, Tokugawa Ieyasu and Oda Nobukatsu waged war against Toyotomi Hideyoshi. The battle ended in a stalemate, but it debilitated the forces of Hideyoshi.

Ieyasu was a clever man and a patient one, and he didn't want Japan to disintegrate into a patchwork of small provinces once again. Therefore, he suggested that Nobukatsu and Hideyoshi resolve their differences, and Ieyasu submitted himself to Hideyoshi as a vassal.

Hideyoshi had an ill-advised dream of uniting China and Japan under his rule. He had engaged in two thwarted attempts to conquer Korea in order to forge the way to China, but he was forced to pull out of there due to illness, letting Ieyasu handle the troops, which he did in 1600 after Hideyoshi's death. To stabilize the future of Japan and avoid a succession crisis since his son was only five years old, Hideyoshi appointed a committee of five members of the most powerful clans, called the Council of the Five Elders, to make administrative decisions regarding the succession. At Fushimi Castle, located at the halfway point between Kyoto and Osaka, Toyotomi Hideyoshi died in 1598. Until they could determine who would be the best ruler to lead a unified Japan, they kept the death of Hideyoshi a secret until 1603. While Tokugawa Ieyasu had been the de facto ruler of Japan since 1600, it wasn't made official until 1603.

The Battle of Sekigahara in 1600: A Humorous Affair

In 1600, Tokugawa Ieyasu had to engage in fighting with the Uesugi clan, whose lands were progressively shrinking. Craving more land, they engaged in rebellions, even after they had been put down multiple times. Ieyasu was residing at Osaka Palace at that time but had to lead his forces out in order to subdue the rebellious Uesugi clan. While he was away, however, the Mori clan along with their warriors, Kobayakawa Hideaki, a nephew of Hideyoshi, Mashita Nagamori, and Ankokuji Ekei, formed an alliance called the Western Army and seized Osaka Palace during Ieyasu's absence. So, Ieyasu formed an alliance with some of the more powerful *daimyos* and retainers like Fukushima Masanori, Ikoma Kazumasa, and Oda Nagamasu, along with his own faithful forces. This was called the Eastern Army.

The two sides were mismatched in terms of numbers. Ishida Mitsunari commanded the Western Army's 120,000 men, while Ieyasu only had 75,000 men. Therefore, this battle would require a great deal of strategy as the unity of Japan was at stake.

There were many misgivings among the fighters and a great reluctance on the part of some clans to fight at all. Some were confident in Ieyasu, while others weren't. Likewise, some of the members of the enemy army had mixed loyalties. As soon as the battle opened, the units under General Otani Yoshitsugu of Ieyasu's Eastern Army fought fiercely but were forced to retreat because they were so badly outnumbered. Mitsunari of the Western Army was a poor leader and had his troops badly formed. So, after Yoshitsugu retreated, it left a huge gap in Mitsunari's forces and essentially split the Western Army into two. That's when Ieyasu's units flew in to fill the gap.

Unfortunately, young Mitsunari had his left flank, mostly those from the Mori clan, placed in the mountains. One of those units, that of Mori Hidemoto, which was 15,000 strong, even sat down to dine! Thus, he didn't join in the battle.

Another Mori clan unit under Hosokawa Yusai deliberately marched so lethargically that they slowed all the other units following them. That gave the clans at the end of the marching column sufficient time to engage in minor skirmishes of their own, rather than staying together with the main Western force.

Kobayakawa Hideaki's unit had initially allied itself with the Western Army, but Hideaki was also wracked with indecision. So, he waited to see how the battle was going and switched sides when he saw Mitsunari's forces become confused and chaotic. As more units of Mitsunari's Western Army became separated, many more members defected to Ieyasu's side.

As could be predicted, Ieyasu and the Eastern Army won the battle.

Ishida Mitsunari, the general of the defeated Western Army, was beheaded in Kyoto. He makes appearances in Clavell's novel, *Shogun*, and the movie, *Sekigahara*, as well as in the video games *Samurai Warriors* and *Nobunaga's Ambition in Japan*.

Chapter 4 – Edo Japan: Part One- 1603 to 1638

The Edo period, or the Tokugawa period, lasted from 1603 to 1868. It was during this time that the Tokugawa shogunate, which Ieyasu founded, ruled Japan. The shogunate was established in the new capital of Edo, which was later called Tokyo.

Ieyasu revised the cuckoo-quote of Nobunaga's and Hideyoshi's to be: "If the cuckoo does not sing, wait for it." Ieyasu was noted for his patience and timing. Like his predecessors before him, he wanted a united Japan; however, he always waited for the opportune time to attend to geopolitical matters. Hideyoshi and Nobunaga both entertained the goal of reuniting Japan and China. Ieyasu, instead, looked after the country and the happiness of its people before considering expansionist policies. He, therefore, postponed the employment of a more aggressive campaign to gain lands, which helped to contribute to the longevity of the Tokugawa era.

Ieyasu looked back at the Muromachi era, during which he had lived, and saw it as a vicious, warring time. It was a time when resentments, bitter rivalries, losses, and sorrows had been visited not only upon the military but also the people. He wanted to reunite Japan and focused his efforts on making that happen by the introduction of diversions and opportunities for cultural and literary advancements.

Even after the Battle of Sekigahara, Ieyasu felt that the private lands of the *daimyos* on both sides shouldn't be confiscated. That would only serve to reignite hostilities and trigger vengeance. So, instead, he divided Japan into domains run by the *daimyos*. Of course, the losing clans moved down a rung on the social hierarchy, and not every clan received what they wanted, but no one went penniless.

Ieyasu also felt that this was a time where arts and culture should be emphasized. He wanted his people to enjoy themselves once again without fear of military raids.

The Edo Pleasure Centers

In Edo, Ieyasu set up what came to be called the "Floating World," named due to the pleasure-seeking lifestyle of Yoshiwara, the red-light district of Edo. Geisha were very popular at this time, although to clear up the common Western misconception, geisha are not prostitutes. While some prostitutes (especially *oiran*, whose attire is similar to that of a geisha) might refer to themselves as a geisha, geisha entertain through dance, art, and singing, depending on more than just sex to entertain male visitors. Chaste teenage girls who danced for pay, called *odoriko*, were also present at this time, but sexual relations weren't permitted with them. Licensed prostitution was permitted, as it was in all of Japan, and homosexuality was also permitted.

Kabuki Performances

Kabuki was a form of theater and dance, somewhat more elaborate that the *noh* style. It was created by Izumo no Okuni, who was a very attractive woman. The actors—who were all female at the beginning—painted their faces white and put on musicals for the most part. Costumes were highly decorated and carefully constructed. Their headdresses were huge, and the players wore many kimonos and capes. Fans were always used and could convey a certain emotion. However, the color blue wasn't used, as it was considered to be negative. Stagehands wore black, so black worn by a performer meant that he was to be regarded as invisible. These performances were very popular in the red-light district in Edo, and women's kabuki was even banned at one point for being too erotic.

As time went on, men began to participate in kabuki. First, adolescent boys performed, but since they were deemed to be suitable for prostitution and often turned toward it, the shogunate banned this form of kabuki as well. So, by the mid-1600s, male kabuki became popular, with men playing both the female and male parts. Kabuki continued to thrive for many years and is still performed today.

Bunraku Puppet Theater

Although this performance uses puppets, *Bunraku* wasn't created for children. *Bunraku* tells a story with a theme that can really only be understood by adults. The puppets are called *ningyo* and have white faces. Chanting or music, either by itself or a combination of the two, is played in the background during these performances and is accompanied by the strumming of a *shamisen*, which is a three-stringed instrument. *Bunraku* is still performed today, and while performances dropped after World War II, it seems as if *Bunraku* has a long history still ahead of it, as more people are becoming interested in preserving this art.

Preservation of the Feudal Structure

The societal structure of Japan became rigid early on in the Tokugawa era, as the country failed to open up relations with other neighboring countries like Korea and China. The internal clan warfare had lessened, so the samurai had virtually little to do except enjoy the pleasure centers and entertainment. As a result, many became impoverished. In order to survive, many samurai slid into the entrepreneurial sector. Those samurai and *daimyos* who couldn't, however, fell into deeper and deeper debt.

The population also increased significantly around the main cities, like Kyoto and Osaka. Merchants took full advantage of that and often overcharged for their goods, thereby increasing the anxiety of the lower classes. Little was left for luxury and even essential items.

To resolve the problems created by the population surge and the money shortage, Ieyasu initiated agrarian projects, like irrigation and fertilization, and increased the amount of farmland available. Cash crops outpaced other crops, and tobacco, grain, sugar cane, rice, cotton, sesame, and spices spurred production. That, in turn, stimulated manufacture related to the use of those plant goods, like rice wine, clothing, weaving, and cotton clothing.

Arrival of Anjin

Ieyasu attempted to keep Japan as isolated as possible, but that principle was broken clandestinely by some of the merchants who traded with pirates. That wasn't the only time this isolation was fractured, however. In 1600, an Englishman by the name of William Adams arrived at the town of Bungo (present-day Usuki). Adams worked for the Dutch East India Company, which was engaged in international trade. When Adams arrived, however, he was sick and feverish, but Adams' presence alarmed the merchants as they didn't want any competition from foreign merchants. So, in an effort to dispose of the problem, the Japanese merchants told Ieyasu that Adams was dishonest. Ieyasu disliked foreigners anyway, so he believed the merchants and threw Adams into prison along with his sickly crew, who were placed in a different cell.

Later on, Ieyasu took Adams out of prison and asked him about the nature of his arrival. Having some familiarity with Asian languages, Adams replied, saying, "We are a people that seek friendship with all nations, and to have trade in all countries, bringing such merchandise as our country did afford into strange lands in the way of traffic." Tokugawa Ieyasu asked a few more general questions but reserved judgment. Concerned about the welfare of his crew, Adams then asked if he could see them. Ieyasu obliged him, and Adams was relieved when he saw that his crew was well and being fairly treated.

After that visit, Adams was thrown back into prison, but later on, Ieyasu asked to meet with him again. During the interview, the shogun asked Adams to build him a ship, as he had seen the remnants of Adams' ship and felt like it might be useful to own one. Adams explained he wasn't a carpenter, but he would do the best he could. With the help of some Japanese craftsmen, Adams built him a fine ship, and Ieyasu was very pleased. The shogun then raised him to the level of a samurai, saying that Williams Adams was dead and that Miura Anjin was born. *Anjin* means pilot and is the nautical term meaning seamen who guide larger ships into ports. This meant that Adams was free to serve the shogunate and made Adams a widow, leaving him no reason to not continue staying in Japan.

In 1605, Ieyasu retired in favor of his son, Tokugawa Hidetada, although he still retained a lot of power in the shogunate. This gave him some time to learn from the Englishman, and they had many discussions. Anjin taught the shogun some basic geometry and mathematics—education he hadn't been exposed to because of Japan's isolationist policies. After that, Ieyasu approved of his son opening up relations with the Dutch East India Company, and later on, in 1613, they opened up the port of Hirado not only to the Dutch but the English and Portuguese as well.

Hidetada permitted more international trading centers to open up in Kyoto, Osaka, Nagasaki, and Edo. Thus, more foreigners came to the country and conducted a great deal of trade. Hidetada and the shoguns who followed him constructed waterways, and eventually highways, to allow for the transportation of goods. Also, more pleasure centers were set up in other major cities.

The integration of the Dutch, English, and Portuguese with the Japanese people was difficult. The foreigners were loud and occasionally rowdy. What's more, they couldn't manage chopsticks and ate with their fingers. The Japanese were horrified at their manners and called them "bar beerean," meaning "barbarians," saying, "They eat with their fingers instead of with chopsticks such as we use. They show their feelings without any self-control."

To maintain peaceful relations and keep the prosperous trade continuing, Hidetada didn't permit the foreign merchants to mingle with the general population in the country, restricting them to the area around Hirado. However, the Portuguese also brought missionaries with them, who had already infiltrated other parts of the country. They did convert some of the Japanese, but they were not a problem to Hidetada until one of his *daimyos*, Arima Harunobu, a Christian convert, became involved in a conspiracy.

Christian Expulsion Edict

After he had lost some lands in the Battle of Sekigahara in 1600, Harunobu bribed an advisor to Ieyasu (who might not have the shogun when these intrigues was taking place but who held much power in the shogunate) to wield influence with the shogunate so he could retrieve some of the fiefs he once owned in the Hinoe Domain. The conspiracy became more entangled when Harunobu schemed with another Christian convert by the name of Okamoto Daihachi to bring that about. When Daihachi didn't follow through, Harunobu tried to get a Jesuit priest to help. That also didn't work, so Harunobu informed Ieyasu about the scheme. Ieyasu became incensed that these Christians were interfering with land redistribution without his permission. In 1612, Ieyasu had Daihachi arrested for his part in the affair and condemned him to execution. When many Christians came to the execution, Ieyasu became furious. This meddling in shogunate affairs caused Ieyasu to forbid Christianity in the entire country. Harunobu was exiled and ordered to commit seppuku after the whole investigation came to light. However, Harunobu indicated that his religion forbade him from committing suicide, so he was beheaded instead.

Ieyasu was especially baffled by the Christians' attendance at executions at which Christian criminals died. In 1614, he once said, "If they see a condemned fellow, they run to him with joy, bow to him, and do him reverence. This they say is the essence of their belief. If this is not an evil law, what is it?"

In June 1616, Tokugawa Ieyasu died, but his son carried on the policies his father had promulgated. More Christian executions followed that one.

The Christian Executions

In 1622, some Catholic missionaries and teachers entered Japan illegally from the Philippines under a Japanese Catholic captain, Joachim. The Dutch traders informed the Japanese governor of Nagasaki, and the ship was captured. They broke out but were captured yet again. The seamen were beheaded, and three more, including Joachim, were burned alive.

The governor then seized 52 Anglican monks who had been imprisoned, along with 30 other prisoners. They were beheaded in the city, including three boys. Thirty converts from Nagasaki were also beheaded or burned at the stake. The Christian persecutions continued from the year 1622 to the year 1637.

Martial Arts

Retired and unemployed former samurai soon realized that the foreigners in their country and even other Japanese wanted to learn martial arts. Dojos, that is, martial arts schools, sprung up around city and town centers. They taught two forms—jujutsu, which uses a short weapon or no weapon at all, and a modified form call kyudo, which uses bows and arrows. Kano Jigoro was a leader in the promotion of the martial arts, not for purposes of war but to highlight the concept he described as making the "most efficient use of mental and physical energy." He eliminated the torturous techniques of eye-gouging and the use of fish hooks to injure an opponent and instead taught his students to learn the art of disrupting an opponent's balance in order to win a bout. Sumo wrestlers, who were probably *ronin* (samurai with no masters) as they needed to find a source of income, also rose in popularity at this time.

Woodblock Art

Ukiyo-e is a type of art created by woodblocks. The term essentially translates to the "pictures of the floating world," the name given to the pleasure palaces. The process called for a number of artisans—the artist who designed it, the craftsman who copied the picture onto wood and cut it, the printer who inked and pressed it onto rice paper or cloth, and the publisher who printed and distributed the work. These beautiful prints were used a great deal to decorate the walls of the Edo pleasure palaces and in the homes of the elite. Japanese writer Asai Ryoi wrote about this art in glowing terms when he described its spirit as "living only for the moment, savoring the moon, the snow, the cherry blossoms, and the maple leaves, singing songs, drinking sake, and diverting oneself just in floating, like a gourd carried along with the river current: this is what we call ukiyo."

Early versions were monochromatic, but later on, color was introduced. Flora, fauna, and landscapes were typical themes. Sometimes the blocks were just of well-executed Japanese writing characters, but they could also be much more elaborate, with the introduction of forms such as women, warriors, and nature. The artisans impressed the blocks on rice paper or cloth and created many prints, even of the same picture. Woodblocks were also used to imprint fine designs on Japanese folding fans.

Ukiyo-e helped to develop the West's perception of Japanese artwork. They were particularly fond of them, so shops opened up around the trading centers.

Haiku

The most famous poet of the 17th century was Matsuo Basho. The haiku, a form of poetry, came into being during this time and was the primary form used by Basho, who is considered to be a master of it. Traditional haiku is composed of seventeen syllables divided into three lines of five syllables, seven syllables, and five syllables. Later on, poets developed variant forms of haiku to accommodate other languages, but they don't stray too far away or at all from the original form. One of Basho's poems follows below.

Furu ike ya

kawazu tobikomu

mizu no oto

(In English:

Breaking the silence

Of an ancient pond,

A frog jumped into the water –

A deep resonance.)

The Shimabara Rebellion

Peace had reigned during most of the reign of the Tokugawa shogunate, but in 1637, an uprising occurred. It didn't originate with the peasants, as might be expected, but with a group of *ronin* against *daimyos* Matsukura Shigemasa's son, Matsukura Katsuie, of the Shimabara Domain and Terasawa Katataka of the Karatsu Domain. The Matsukuras built a magnificent palace for themselves, with more construction soon to follow. However, the people and the samurai didn't have the money to finance such undertakings due to famine and over taxation. The Catholic peasants from the Arima clan, dismantled under Hideyoshi's former reign, also joined the rebellion under the leadership of Amakusa Shiro to protest the ban on Christianity.

The rebel forces stationed themselves at Hara Castle in the Nagasaki region of southern Japan. After more discontented people joined in, their forces grew to about 40,000 men. The Tokugawa shogunate was alarmed, as their own armies were beginning to be outnumbered, and the rebellion looked like it might drag on for many months. Therefore, the shogunate under Tokugawa Iemitsu, the grandson of Ieyasu, sought the support of the Dutch traders. The Dutch were mostly Protestants, who opposed the Catholics, and they could also provide armaments, gunpowder, and cannons. With this, the shogunate forces possessed an overwhelming advantage.

The rebels were forced to retreat to their headquarters at Hara Castle in April of 1638. They erected fortifications and redoubts to prevent entry. The shogun's forces tore down the fortifications and bombarded the castle, surrounding it. When the rebels ran out of supplies, one of their leaders, Yamada Emosaku, betrayed that fact to the shogunate, and the castle was overrun. Amakusa Shiro was beheaded, and his head was displayed in the predominantly Catholic town of Nagasaki. The castle was then burned along with all the bodies of the dead. Today, many tourists travel to this site to view the ruins of this once impressive castle.

Because many of the Portuguese traders were Catholics and their arrival included Jesuit missionaries, Portugal was forbidden to trade with Japan and had to leave. A huge population loss also occurred in Shimabara due to this revolt, and immigrants from other areas of Japan were invited into the region in order to save the rice harvest.

As could be predicted, the ban against Christianity was tightened, and the remaining Christians were forced to publicly renounce their faith. Many of the Christians, however, sought refuge underground, becoming what was known as "hidden Christians."

Chapter 5 – Edo Period: Part Two- 1638 to 1868

Isolationism to Internationalism

After the Shimabara Rebellion, the Tokugawa clan receded within itself and made Japan an isolated country. They were oversensitive to foreign influence, and most broke relations with their trade partners within the country itself. Gradually, the shogun Tokugawa Iemitsu increased Japan's isolationist policy by passing a series of edicts between the years 1633 and 1639 called *sakoku*. Foreigners were not permitted entry into the country, and the common Japanese people were not permitted to leave under penalty of death. In fact, the Japanese merchants who were living abroad most of the year suddenly found themselves spending their lives in another country. This policy lasted for over 220 years, only ending after 1853 when trade was opened up to America.

As these mandates were being passed, the foreign traders were leaving, with the exception of the Dutch and the Dutch East India Company. They were told to relocate their trading houses to Dejima, a manmade island in the port of Nagasaki. For all intents and purposes, though, they were imprisoned there.

The Genroku era started in late 1688 and ended toward the beginning of 1704. The emperor at this time was Higashiyama, and the shogun was Tokugawa Tsunayoshi. The Japanese minister, Matsudaira Sadanobu, instituted many reforms. Under this leadership, agricultural, urban, and population growth increased and expanded. That set the stage toward internationalism and societal progress. One of the vanguard companies in that is the famous Mitsui corporation. Mitsui started out as a humble little clothing shop in 1673 under the name Mitsikoshi but exploded into a textile firm and then an international lending group.

All of the social classes had grown weary of their self-imposed suffering under outdated isolationism. The peasants were still highly taxed and couldn't share in the greater wealth created by a proliferation of crops. Merchants could conduct their businesses and amass great wealth, but they lacked political power and couldn't contribute to decisions related to their own function in society, which was to trade with the world. The larger landowners split their lands into smaller holdings farmed by one family or clan, and in time, each of the smaller landowners became more powerful. The *daimyos* and shoguns again became wealthy from the lands they were awarded by virtue of their military accomplishments; however, they but lacked purpose as there were no more wars to be fought. The samurai and military men had little cash flow and enormous debts. They were the most stagnant of all the social castes but were not quiet about it.

Edo Fires

Many *daimyos* chose to maintain a residence in Edo, as well as one in his own province, which also meant that a large number of samurai were housed in Edo as well. Not only that, but merchants and artisans moved to Edo in droves, creating a large population boom. Because of that, more residences, most of which were shabby, needed to be built for the people performing in the theater, as well as dancers, geisha, and other performers. Houses were built close together (although the *daimyos* and samurai enjoyed a bit more space than the other classes), and the paper and wood building materials made the spreading of a possible fire even easier. It would not take much heat to ignite a vigorous fire.

Also, at this time, it did not help that fire regulations were nearly nonexistent. They did have a crude city fire extinguisher, but it wasn't large enough to stop the spreading of a large blaze. There were no trained firemen. Actually, most of the firemen were steeplejacks, men who would climb great heights to carry out repairs, and they would use the fire to show off their skills, spreading the flames in the process.

The winds in Edo were changeable due to the meteorological conditions in the country, as they could carry the fires far and wide. The passageways between the buildings only enhanced this problem, as they were narrow enough to create "wind tunnels" between the flimsily constructed buildings.

In 1657, there was the Great fire of Meireki that destroyed between sixty to seventy percent of Edo. Legend has it that a temple priest had started it by burning a cursed kimono! However, it is entirely possible that it started by accident or was the cause of arson. The problem of arson was so severe during the 17th century that arson was punishable by death. However, as the shogunate grew more unstable, arson only increased.

Earthquake and the Great Eruption of Mount Fuji

Geological events broke the Japanese cocoon of isolation wide open during the Edo era because of the fires in Edo, a huge earthquake in Osaka in November of 1707, and the eruption of Mount Fuji in December of the same year. The earthquake, known as the Hoei earthquake, was the strongest earthquake in Japanese history until 2011. The quake itself, as well as the tsunami that it triggered, caused more than 5,000 casualties and destroyed 29,000 houses.

Besides starting the tsunami, some believe the earthquake also triggered the eruption of Mount Fuji by disrupting the magma layer underneath the ground, causing compression of the area containing the liquid magma. As the magma flowed underground, it mingled with the other magma already under Mount Fuji. The two magmas had different consistencies, thereby creating a more intense eruption called a Plinian eruption, which is named after Pliny the Younger, who described it in a letter after the eruption of Mount Vesuvius in 79 CE. Magma continued to collect under Mount Fuji, building up pressure before the pyroclastic expulsions caused huge rocks to spew high into the air, while the towns and buildings below were covered with deep ash. The air was full of this black smoke, making it so that even the sun could not be seen, and people had to evacuate.

There were a number of smaller intermittent quakes at first on the southeastern slope of Mount Fuji before the pyroclastic blast happened. Thousands of people and their homes were destroyed. In the end, the whole southwestern side of Mount Fuji was gone, leaving the Hoei crater in its place.

Survival Overcomes Stagnation

Recovery from geological disasters can be viewed as challenging interruptions in the ordinary course of life, and the eruption of Mount Fuji served as a wake-up call. Japan was practically asleep due to its isolationism, but the psychological impact of this eruption drew the people's attention to the fact that change was needed. Adaptation to changing circumstances was essential to Japan's survival as a nation in the ever-evolving world.

The Japanese during the Genroku era of the Tokugawa shogunate signaled the beginning of the end of the vestiges of the old Tokugawa era. Modern Japan was emerging, regardless of any of the efforts to hold onto feudalism. The peasants had staged uprising after uprising. The samurai, who found themselves virtually unemployed, rose up and destroyed their adherence to their previous way of life, shaking off the shackles of the military subcultures. They were impoverished by the lack of wars and no longer wanted to wage them anyway. Instead, they moved into other areas like entrepreneurship, the teaching of martial arts, and mercantilism. Some even became bureaucrats who had some power within the government.

Even the contemplative Buddhists moved into the world of social change. During the Shimabara Rebellion in 1637, monks fought alongside peasants and *ronin*, and commoners fought alongside samurai and Buddhists.

The infrastructure was also in place for the coming of modern Japan—there were railways, roads, and huge expanding urban centers. Farms were irrigated, and crops were produced and shipped not only within the country but outside of it as well.

Japanese Copper Cracks Opens the Japanese Door to the World

During the Edo Period, the Chinese and Koreans discovered that Japanese copper was far superior to that of China. In the interest of a source of newfound wealth, the sequestered shogunate broke its long-standing tradition of isolationism. The export of copper from Japan to China and Korea resulted in an exchange of learning that infiltrated Japan. This learning not only helped them hone their copper trade but other skills as well. In addition, Chinese texts and literature reached Japan, and commerce began to thrive.

The beginning of a large company started out investing in this raw material. In 1615, a Buddhist monk named Sumitomo Masatomo opened a bookshop to spread the teachings of Buddhism but then invested in the mining of copper. Today, it is known as the Sumitomo Group, which is a large financial investment firm.

The Forty-Seven Ronin

Japan's bond to each clan during the feudal times grew more intense due to their isolation. The samurai were expected to be loyal to their *daimyo* until they died. In the year 1701, Kamei Korechika and Asano Naganori, both shogunate officials, were ordered to prepare a reception for Kira Yoshinaka, a powerful official in the shogunate of Tokugawa Tsunayoshi. The celebration was held in the sacred town of Edo, and gifts were arranged, but they were judged to be inadequate by Yoshinaka, who complained bitterly. Naganori withstood this dressing-down stoically, but Yoshinaka continued to harass and insult him. At one point, Naganori lost his temper, drew a sword, and cut into Yoshinaka's flesh. The wound was only minor, but Yoshinaka took extreme offense. It was against the code of honor to draw a sword in Edo, and Yoshinaka was unforgiving and demanded that Asano Naganori commit seppuku.

He did so, leaving his estates to be divided up among the other lords and leaving behind 47 unemployed samurai, who would become *ronin* after his death. The leader of the *ronin*, Oishi Yoshio, who was usually drunk, swore revenge upon Kira Yoshinaka for this merciless killing. Oishi persuaded his men to attack, and for two years, they carefully planned an attack on Yoshinaka's residence with the intention of killing him as well. They found Yoshinaka, who was hiding in an inner chamber, and they told him their intentions, that they came as true samurai to avenge the death of their master, and offered Yoshinaka the death of a true samurai: seppuku. However, Yoshinaka was too scared to talk, and Oishi commanded his men to pin him down before he cut off his head.

It was illegal to carry out such an act of vengeance in Edo, but they did so anyway to avenge their master, Naganori, which was totally acceptable according to the precepts of the samurai. The shogunate officials met on the issue and sentenced the *ronin* to death. However, to come to a compromise, the *ronin* were asked to commit seppuku rather than undergo a criminal execution. They did so with great ceremony, which symbolized their loyalty, persistence, sacrifice, and honor. This tale had been told and retold throughout the centuries in plays, movies, and books.

Kyoho Reforms 1736

While Confucian teachings permeated the Japanese mind and spirit, Confucianism stressed the unimportance of money. Of course, money is essential to propel an economy forward, and those Confucian ideals in practice were unrealistic in a growing country with an expanding population. Wisely, the governmental administers made reforms that allowed for the greater growth of the merchant guilds, as well as the lifting of sanctions on reading Chinese and foreign books that could be used to expand skills, medical techniques, and the sciences. Attention was paid to more efficient agricultural methods, including the opening of the Dojima Rice Exchange. This gave rise to a securities market as well. It was, however, vulnerable to conditions in the market, and prices sometimes fell. However, that encouraged workers to develop other skills and products.

Monetization was introduced, especially since the discovery of copper gave the people an unbiased means of exchange. During this time, a rule was implemented that stated that every *daimyo* had to maintain two residences—one in his home community and one in Edo. That practice was eliminated, as it required not only the *daimyos* to maintain two homes but also carried the expectation that he must travel in style to Edo with long festive parades of followers carrying all the accouterments of celebration.

The Horeki River Incident

In 1754, a system of dams was proposed by the central government for the areas that tended to flood precious farmlands. Initially, the supervision of the project was awarded to the *daimyo* of the Satsuma prefecture. Clan rivalries erupted over that decision but were suppressed. Those who disliked the Tokugawa shogun, who was Ieshige, sabotaged the project, too. In addition to that drawback, the rising costs of this project led to severe periods of food shortages. Because of Japan's isolation, which deprived them of the knowledge of skills related to flood control, the project wasn't that effective.

However, it did indicate the great need to make some improvements. Those were actually done during the next era, known as the Meiji Restoration period.

The Kansei Reforms

The Kansei Reforms were basically programs that set the course of growth in the reverse direction. They were engineered by a stateman named Matsudaira Sadanobu, the chief counselor to the shogun, Tokugawa Ienari. His program advocated a return to stricter obedience to the principles of Confucianism. Foreign books were prohibited, and foreign merchants were severely restricted. Japanese merchants who generally traveled abroad were prohibited from doing so. In fact, some of them were abroad at the time, and when these reforms came into practice in 1787, they were stranded in those other countries until the end of the reforms in 1793.

Isolation Broken

Japan was seen as an opportune location to conduct trade by the rest of the world. The fact that they had deep-water ports alone was tempting to foreign traders. The few foreigners who had gained legal entry for diplomatic and other reasons provided fodder for other countries to initiate projects to open up the country. Even Chinese pirates that illegally traded with Japanese junks off the coasts carried tales of the wealth of raw materials and products that could not only boost the local economy of southeast Asia but also boost the development of Japan.

"Black Ships of Evil Mien"[1]

However, the policy of sakoku, which denied foreigners entry to the country and common Japanese to leave it, didn't end with this opening up of trade. Many attempts were made throughout the years, but the ending of the policy was thanks to Commodore Matthew Perry of the US Navy, who arrived in Yokosuka, located south of

---

[1] *Mien*, when translated, means appearance.

Edo, with four warships in June 1853. The initial reaction of the startled Japanese sword-toting samurai in crude wooden ships was fear. They called this never-before-seen armada as "black" and "evil," which led to the ships being called the Black Ships. With the arrival of the Black Ships, the Japanese suddenly realized they had no defenses for such a force. It was a rude awakening for the shogunate.

The United States had just settled in the state of California and wanted some way to curtail the total European monopoly of the Pacific Ocean. Opening up Japan to world trade would be the best way to do so. Perry was sent by US President Millard Fillmore to do just that, even being given the authorization to use gunboat diplomacy if needed.

When Perry arrived in Yokosuka, he ordered his ships to turn their guns toward the city, ignoring any demands to leave or sail to Nagasaki, the only port open to foreigners. Attempting to intimidate them, Perry sent them a white flag and a letter which stated that if they chose to fight against his forces, the United States would destroy them.

At the time, Tokugawa Ieyoshi was sick, so there was no one in charge to make such a big decision. In July, a senior councilor decided to accept Perry's letter, who was allowed to land on shore a few days later. After giving them the letter, Perry told the delegates that he would be back the following year for their reply. The letter stated:

> Great and good friend: I send you this public letter by Commodore Matthew Perry visiting your imperial majesty's dominions. I have directed Commodore Perry to assure your imperial majesty that I entertain the kindest feelings towards your majesty's person and government, and that I have no other object in sending him to Japan but to propose to your imperial majesty the United States and Japan should live in friendship and have commercial intercourse with each other.

As a point of powerful persuasion, Perry's letter made mention of the fact that only China, Korea, and the Dutch were permitted to trade with Japan. As an incentive, the letter indicated that the United States had goods that were desirable in Japan, such as gold, precious stones, silver, and quicksilver. The letter also stated that the United States would be interested in buying coal from the Japanese for their steamships, along with water and provisions.

The shogun and the top leaders of the Tokugawa shogunate had already decided to accept the American offer. However, members of the ruling clans argued about where to hold talks with the Americans, thus delaying the entire process of negotiating a treaty. Finally, Yokohama was the site chosen, and a building was erected to handle the affair.

The Treaty of Kanagawa

Commodore Perry returned to Japan in February 1854, not even granting the Japanese the full year he had promised. This time, he arrived with a large fleet of ten ships and 1,600 men. After some initial resistance, Perry was allowed to land at Kanagawa, near present-day Yokohama, on March 8th. Hayashi Akira was the Japanese representative of the imperial court who spoke with Perry. After about a month of negotiations, the treaty was signed on March 31st, 1854, with the understanding that more treaties would follow. The treaty stipulated that Japan would 1) permit American access to the ports of Shimoda and Hakodate, 2) the Japanese would assist any shipwrecked American sailors if necessary, 3) American ships would purchase provisions from Japan exclusively, 4) America would open up a consulate in Shimoda, and 5) another official treaty would be drawn up delineating further details.

After the Kanagawa Convention, the United States gifted Japan with a model steam locomotive, a telegraph device, agricultural apparatuses, whiskey, clocks, stoves, and books about the US. The Japanese gave the Americans bronze ornaments, furniture decorated with gold lacquer, porcelain items, Japanese goblets, and a seashell collection in honor of Commodore Perry.

Although the negotiations ended peacefully, and Emperor Komei ratified it the following year, the treaty was not actually valid. The shogun, who held the actual power in Japan, did not sign the treaty nor did his representatives. However, that was a point that never really came up since more treaties were signed with the Americans and other foreigners.

The Harris Treaty

In 1858, Townsend Harris, an American diplomat, met with Japanese officials to negotiate a revised treaty called the Treaty of Amity and Commerce, also known as the Harris Treaty. This treaty opened up more ports to America in addition to Shimoda and Hakodate—Nagasaki, Kanagawa, Niigata, and Hyogo. The Americans were permitted religious freedom, duties on exports and imports of Japanese and American products were to be charged, Japan was granted a "most-favored-nation" status by America, and trade representatives were allowed to reside in the aforementioned port cities.

Within five years, Japan had signed treaties with other Western countries. However, these treaties were often unfair to the Japanese. For instance, the Ansei Treaties, which were signed with the United States, the United Kingdom, the Netherlands, France, and Russia, were seen by the Japanese as a way to force imperialism onto their country. Japan gave these nations control of the tariffs on the imports, and their diplomats were exempt from Japanese laws. Some Japanese chalked these unfair terms up to the use of gunboat diplomacy, which was the threat of war if a country did not agree with the more superior power.

End of the Tokugawa Shogunate

Horrendous disagreements arose between two domains, Satsuma and Choshu, when the Tokugawa shogunate failed to oppose the exposure of Japan to the outside world. Those two provinces delayed the signing of foreign treaties, and even some of the samurai were actively preaching a return to isolation in order to preserve their old system of individual shogunates and adherence to traditional practices. That only provoked the Japanese peasants and the tradesmen whose businesses could not expand without these treaties.

The more realistic samurai had come to the realization that it would be impossible for Japan to stop progress. When Sir Harry Parkes of the United Kingdom visited Japan in 1865 to negotiate a treaty, he deliberately avoided approaching the emperor's court and went directly to the country's judicial seat in Kyoto. When the counselors of the *daimyo* who held control of the ultra-conservative provinces of Satsuma and Choshu went to England, however, they reversed their position on isolationism. They realized that the traditional approach of the Tokugawa shogunate was ineffective in the 19th-century world.

In 1866, Tokugawa Iemochi died. He had wanted a return to tradition but was unable to make that happen, which shows that the shogunate was greatly weakened by this point. His successor was Tokugawa Yoshinobu, and many of the older traditional samurai expected him to follow their instructions and reinstate the isolationist policies of the past.

Yoshinobu actually seemed like he was headed the right way; he built up the shogunate, strengthening the army, navy, and government. But the Satsuma and Choshu Provinces, along with the province of Tosa, feared his growing power. It was clear that people were ready for a change, and even the emperor began issuing orders that the shogunate would have been responsible for in earlier years. For instance, Emperor Komei's "Order to Expel Barbarians" in 1863 was actually followed through, which even prompted attacks on the shogunate.

Although the shogunate might have seemed to be on the right path toward being the dominant power once again, the conditions in Japan just were not right for that to happen. The alliance of the three provinces wanted the shogun to be killed (although, to be fair, the Tosa Province just wanted him to resign). Yoshinobu actually did resign before any major trouble happened in 1867, leaving the power of the shogunate in the hands of the emperor.

Chapter 6 – The Meiji Restoration

The Meiji period, which lasted from 1868 to 1912, was a turning point in Japan. It was both politically and socially traumatic. After the conservatives from the Satsuma and Choshu Provinces had returned from their visit to England in 1866, a radical change had occurred. Reformers arose from within the Satsuma and Choshu areas, and their military advisors recommended that Emperor Komei and his son, Prince Mutsuhito, challenge the Tokugawa shogunate and restore prestige to the imperial line. After Komei's death, Prince Mutsuhito was renamed Emperor Meiji, and Edo was renamed "Tokyo."

A need to reform Japan's antiquated economic and administrative top-down structure was critical, and rapid political and social changes started to take place. Fukuzawa Yukichi, an accomplished scholar, visited Europe and founded Keio University, located in Tokyo.

Japan was a country that respected its heritage but didn't object to some extraneous modifications in areas that wouldn't revolutionize the country in all its facets, and in the 1870s, a more pragmatic approach prevailed. Confucianism supported the fact that the elites in society should be involved with the administrative functions and that the country should be run by senior bureaucrats who were more familiar with how the state should function.

Confucius also stated that mercantilism was a "dirty" but necessary profession, so those who worked in commerce were considered to be people who were not as bright as those who chose other professions. To rectify this, the finance minister, Matsukata Masayoshi, established some privatization of national industries. As it was, some were unprofitable, but private entrepreneurs could convert those organizations into useful entities.

Under these ideals, a new progressive government was formed. As part of the reforms, the Charter Oath was passed. It was designed to cushion the blow of sudden traumatic changes by incorporating more democratic ideals. The Charter Oath consisted of the creation of national assemblies, the involvement of all social classes in Japanese affairs, the search for international knowledge rather than just Japanese history, and the ceasing of "evil customs." "Evil customs" referred to the required customs, such as a topknot and a long braid, to distinguish between a samurai and a peasant, respectively. They were called "evil" to inform even the ignorant that these practices were from the past and would cause derision toward those who kept up with these old customs. Accouterments of that type were reserved for costumes, ceremonies, and historical depictions.

End of the Feudal System

The feudal social system was abolished in 1871 with the surrender of the *daimyo* estates. No one was locked into living in a particular class for their entire life. Lands owned by the *daimyos* were "surrendered" to the emperor in the form of nationalization. No longer were the domains controlled by the former Tokugawa *daimyos* considered their personal property; the land was instead divided into prefectures and subdivisions. The former *daimyos* either continued to rule over the lands, who were now regarded as governors, or they were given generous pensions and retired. The military was no longer driven by the samurai, and mandated military service was required of all able-bodied males in their twenties.

The merchants fared the best during this change, despite the fact that they were once considered the lowest class. They were enabled to grow their businesses, and many were financially stable, having granted loans to the samurai and other influential members of society. The Sumitomo Group, the aforementioned copper mining company established during the Tokugawa era, was now able to take advantage of Western technologies and extract copper more inexpensively. Not only that, but it later adopted processes for deriving silver from copper ore. The Sumitomo Group was also involved in the import-export business and opened up a silk business. The new freedoms established during the Meiji period helped the company expand into banking, coal, warehousing, and financial investment. The Mitsui corporation, which also found its origins during the Tokugawa period, opened a large bank during this period. Today, it has about ten corporate subsidiaries.

One of the reasons for the term "Meiji Restoration" refers to the fact that the emperor was "restored" to a supreme position in the country rather than a shogun, like Tokugawa Ieyasu or Tokugawa Hidetada, holding the power. A constitutional form of government seemed to be compatible with the country, which had been accustomed to a central government with a solitary leader and a workable system where everyone had some degree of representation. There were, however, a number of limitations on what is today considered to be democratic freedoms. In terms of voting, only males 25 years old or older who paid at least 15 yen in taxes were allowed to vote. That limited the number of legal voters to only one percent of the population.

Japan had a functioning system of justice since the Heian period but updated it through the establishment of the Ministry of Justice in the Meiji period. Criminal justice encompassed the administration of trials and the imposition of penalties. There were five different courts: the Supreme Court, high courts, district courts, family courts, and summary (martial law) courts. The new administrative government was composed of the office of Civil Affairs to handle internal affairs, foreign affairs, the army, the navy, the imperial household, the Department of Justice, public work projects, and education.

There had also been little attention paid to the important role of the military during the prior era, and there was very little instituted by way of technological improvements. For instance, transportation during the isolated Tokugawa period was primitive. The antiquated use of ox carts, palanquins (a litter carried by people), or boats on the water were the traditional ways to get from one place to another. To catch up with the rest of the developed world, a railway line was laid between Tokyo and Yokohama, as well as between Osaka and Kyoto. In 1868, Thomas Blake Glover, a Scottish merchant, introduced "Iron Duke," a steam locomotive, to Nagasaki. This innovation was extremely useful in getting products to and from international destinations, and British financiers provided the funding for the project. In 1871, Edmund Morei, a British engineer, was instrumental in the construction of another railroad on the island of Honshu. Hermann Rumschottel, a German engineer, supervised the construction of a railway system in Kyushu. Two more lines were financed by the Japanese government and connected the major cities of Japan to each other and were serviced by the Nippon Railway Company.

Education in the Tokugawa shogunate was limited to the elite classes, with schools devoted to the martial arts for the samurai. With the heralding of the Meiji period, education was made compulsory, and a new system was founded based on the American and French systems. In 1890, Emperor Meiji passed the "Imperial Rescript on Education," which presented the basic precepts of education for the country. Initial recommendations promoted Confucian ideals of conformity and obedience to imperial authority, but the more liberal leaders modified it to allow for greater democracy, personal responsibility, and societal morality. With the aid of advisors, the Meiji administration set up schools in Buddhist temples, as well as other places for non-Buddhists. The old feudal schools to train the samurai were converted by the former *daimyos*, who were now functioning as governors, and became middle schools. During the Tokugawa period, there was an imperial school run by the shogunate staff, but this was transformed into what would become the University of Tokyo.

Reformation of the military was greatly enhanced by the recommendations of former samurai as well as civic leaders. Three years of military service was compulsory, and the Meiji adopted a Prussian model for its structure and even adopted modern weaponry. After some resistance, the samurai were coaxed to transfer loyalties they once felt for their shoguns to the emperor and the feudal landlords. A central office, the Imperial Japanese Army General Staff Office, oversaw the newly formed army. Shipbuilders were recruited, some of whom were foreign, and Japan worked diligently at building up a navy.

Governmental Reorganization

After the Satsuma Rebellion of 1877, which was really more of a civil war and will be discussed in more detail at the beginning of the next chapter, the government felt that they had exerted their control over the population. Emphasis was then placed on reinforcing internal stability, which set the stage for the establishment of governmental bodies. Modernization of industry, which had, to some extent, already started, continued to flourish. Cartels were formed to control particular industries, and

politics were relegated to the leaders supported by a staff of administrators. Because the Satsuma, Choshu, and Tosa people were the first to institute the break-up of the Tokugawa shogunate, they became the most powerful people in Japan, relegating many of the administrative posts to themselves. Since Japan was completely overhauling the government, early efforts tended to be directed toward eliminating the abuses of the Tokugawa era and designing a substitute framework for the social classes. Therefore, changes were disorganized and in the hands of a small number of people.

The "Freedom and People's Rights Movement" was a grassroots group, the purpose of which was to prevent the central government from becoming an association of a small group of people, mostly those from the Satsuma and Choshu Provinces. This movement was an effort to gain a voice in the formation of a new government.

New Trend: Political Parties

Various influential political leaders battled for supremacy in the formation of this new government. Of course, the entire country started out with no model for a coordinated approach. It was a collection of voices, each with its own agenda.

The Public Society for Patriots

To establish a direction, though, leaders arose, and political parties were formed. The first party was called the Public Society for Patriots, also called the "Liberal Party," and it was founded by Itagaki Taisuke, Chiba Takusaburo, Eto Shimpei, and Goto Shojiro.

Two of the political figures that initiated this party were Itagaki Taisuke and Chiba Takusaburo. One of the most important goals of this party was the writing of a constitution, with Chiba Takusaburo drafting one. Chiba wasn't the only person to advocate a constitution, though.

This party was formed in 1874 and can be considered to be the first political party of Japan. Although the party lost steam along the way, Taisuke revived it in the 1890s.

The Constitutional Progressive Party

In 1882, Okuma Shigenobu created a governmental structure similar to the British parliamentary system and also presented the Meiji central body with a constitution. He called the central government a "Diet" with a legislative body that was bi-cameral, consisting of a House of Peers and a House of Representatives. The House of Peers were nobles or from the imperial family. The House of Representatives was restricted to males who paid a certain amount of taxes.

The Constitutional Imperial Rule Party

This party was conservative in nature and was founded in 1882 by Fukuchi Gen'ichiro. It supported a constitutional monarchy with a constitution, but they wanted to limit freedom of speech and the right to assemble freely.

The Rikken Seiyukai Party

This party, called "Seiyukai," for short, was a latecomer, being founded in 1900. Although Seiyukai ostensibly advertised itself as "liberal," it was relatively conservative. The origins of this party stemmed from businesses seeking to protect themselves by running pro-business candidates for offices in the Diet.

The Kenseito Party

In 1898, this party was formed under the leadership of Okuma Shigenobu, who had headed the short-lived Shimpoto party, and Itagaki Taisuke, who led the Constitutional Liberal Party (what was once the Public Society for Patriots). However, it almost disintegrated after Okuma failed to come through with his promises when he was made a prime minister. It managed to restructure itself, though, forming the New Kenseito with Itagaki at the head.

For the remainder of the Meiji Restoration, there was a proliferation of political parties and mergers and offshoots of them. For example, the Chugoku Progressive Party established in 1894, spun off the Liberal Democratic Party, the Constitutional Democratic Party, and the Democratic Party for the People, and it later formed the Shimpoto party.

The Meiji Constitution

Ito Hirobumi, a prominent Japanese politician, was commissioned by the central government to draw up a constitution in 1890. It was similar to Okuma Shigenobu's British-style model, and it also drew inspiration from the Prusso-German model. The Prusso-German facet of it utilized the concept of an absolute monarchy combined with a parliamentary structure. The emperor was the sovereign head of state. He had a Cabinet, a privy council, a judicial arm, a legislative group called the "Diet," and a military arm. It should be noted that while the emperor was seen as the head of state, the prime minister (who was voted in by the privy council) was seen as the head of government.

The emperor was considered to be of divine ancestry "unbroken for ages eternal." This was something that dated back to the beginning of Japanese history, and although the emperors lost power when the shogunates rose, they were still fairly well respected by the people. Now that they had gained the power back, the constitution wanted to ensure that there would be limitations to his power. They did this with two articles: he was limited to the provisions of the constitution, and he had to get the signature from one of his ministers of state before an edict or mandate could go into effect. However, the emperor had the right to dismiss a minister of state, so, in a sense, the emperor retained enormous control. This approach did have the effect of solidifying the power of the elites, though.

The emperor's people had some rights, including the freedom of movement, that is, the right to move one's residence; the freedom from unwarranted search or entry; the privacy of correspondence; the right to own personal property; and the freedom of speech.

First Elections

The Japanese had been acclimated to responding to the leadership of one person and his advisors. This trend continued into the Meiji period. Although there were many political parties, the Japanese tended to follow a particular leader and all but disregard the policies the parties advocated.

The first election was held in 1890. The most influential politicians of the time were Itagaki Taisuke and Okuma Shigenobu. Their parties won the majority of the votes in the House of Representatives, as expected. When the first prime minister, Yamagata Aritomo, recommended that the House support the central government in enacting meaningful change, it ignored him. Instead, they voted to cut the budget of the administration, starting with steep salary cuts. The central administration retaliated by resorting to intimidation, including threats from gangsters. Then Itagaki made a secret agreement with the prime minister and shocked his supporters by proposing a six percent, rather than a ten percent, cut in administrative salaries. When Yamagata left his position, it was filled by his protégé, and nothing new was proposed. Instead, more budgetary cuts were passed, including the expenses involved with forming a new navy and a shipbuilding program.

The central government was furious and dissolved the Diet. A special election was held in 1892, but it was violent, with four hundred people being killed. Stubbornly, the newly elected House didn't make any changes to the proposed budget. Because the budget was insufficient to build up the military, the emperor made a huge monetary contribution to military expenditures and recommended that other Cabinet members do the same. They did so, and the Diet then reinstated the original budgetary proposal and moved on from there to foreign affairs.

Economic Advances

Once the feudal collar had been loosened, the mercantile sector expanded more rapidly than the conservatives in government could control. The budgetary restraints after the first and second elections forced the central government to let the mercantile sector expand. Japanese conglomerates banded together, forming what is known as *zaibatsu*, in reaction to excessive governmental interference. Although the term didn't become common until after World War I, their power started in the Meiji period, and they controlled significant chunks of the economy until the end of World War II.

Once the government realized that they could utilize these companies to assume duties in procuring military equipment and building ships for the expanding Japanese navy, they created agreements so the companies could do so.

The Meiji era had followed the model set down centuries ago, where a large number of people and entities were controlled by the few. For example, the Satsuma and Choshu prefectures had huge control over the entire company, much like the shogunates, who virtually ran Japan with a handful of powerful leaders.

Chapter 7 – Foreign Relations

Ganghwa Incident

Japan wanted to open up relations with Korea, so they sent a letter to the king in 1868; however, they used the incorrect Chinese characters to talk about the Japanese emperor. At the time, only the Chinese emperor was allowed to use those symbols, and Japan using them made it seem like they were claiming their emperor was equal to China's. The Chinese suggested the Koreans accept the letter regardless, knowing the power Japan now held, but the old school Koreans refused to do so, and tensions grew.

In September 1875, the Meiji administration sent over the *Un'yo*, a gunboat, to Korea. The crew stopped on Ganghwa Island, asking for water and provisions. Suddenly, the Korean gun batteries opened fire on them, and Japan responded with volleys of loud gunfire on their fort. The Japanese soldiers landed, and a skirmish broke out. Because the Korean weaponry was outdated, the Japanese were able to kill 35 of them. Once the causes behind the incident were straightened out, the Joseon dynasty in Korea quickly drew up a proposed treaty, as they could see the superiority of the Japanese equipment and its forces. The Treaty of Ganghwa was signed in late February 1876, and it contained an apology, just as the Japanese had requested. The treaty opened up Korea to Japanese trade.

The Satsuma Rebellion

The most traumatic result of the abolition of the feudal system was the automatic loss of jobs for the samurai. Suddenly, they were robbed of a lifestyle they had had for the majority of their lives, and the short-sighted new government did a poor job of creating new employment opportunities for them.

In 1876, an activist named Saigo Takamori, a former samurai, concocted a scheme to trigger a war with Korea, thus creating a need for Japan to keep its samurai. Saigo was so committed to this cause that he decided to scapegoat himself by getting the Koreans to kill him. He did this by resurrecting an argument over a protocol faux-pas that occurred during the Ganghwa Incident. However, the imperial government discovered the conspiracy and prevented it from happening.

After that, Saigo built paramilitary academies full of highly motivated students. The Meiji government was concerned about Saigo's popularity and his following, so they had weapons removed from a local arsenal to prevent a raid. The students retaliated by removing weapons from a different arsenal, and sporadic skirmishes resulted. Saigo was astonished by the fervor of his following, and encouraged by this fact, he led a rebellion against the central government.

In 1877, his forces set siege upon Kumamoto Castle in Japan. When no significant headway was made by the rebels, more ex-samurai joined the ranks, and the Saigo supporters grew to be around 25,000 men. Under the leadership of Lieutenant General Tani Tateki, the imperial army, which numbered close to 100,000 (a vast difference between Saigo's forces, but Saigo had much more experienced men in his ranks), held off Saigo's warriors. When more imperial forces arrived, Saigo's supporters were forced to retreat. Saigo and his warriors then moved to Kagoshima in the southern prefecture of Kyushu. Despite the fact that Saigo sent a letter to the imperial forces offering to negotiate and end the hostilities, the government was determined to brutally suppress this rebellion. Instead of discussing terms, the Meiji government increased its numbers and backed the imperial forces up with a warship, pommeling the remaining rebels with volleys of firepower. Toward the very end of the fighting, only forty men remained under Saigo.

During the battle, Saigo was injured in the hip. Some accounts state that he committed seppuku or was assisted in his suicide, but some scholars think that Saigo actually went into shock from his wound and that his followers, upon seeing his impaired state, cut off his head. If this was the case, they would have later said that he committed seppuku to preserve his honor. Whatever the case may be, Saigo's death brought an end to the rebellion.

The Imo Incident

The Chinese indicated that Korea should exercise caution when Russia and the United States approached to open relations with them. In an unexpected move, the United States signed the Treaty of Peace, Amity, Commerce and Navigation, also known as the Shufeldt Treaty. However, the treaty identified Korea as an independent country, which wasn't China's understanding. When Korea definitively eliminated its status as a tributary state of China, this concerned Japan, as it meant that China might not rush to Korea's defense in case of an attack. Because Korea wasn't militarily prepared to defend itself against attacks, Japan felt like that would leave them vulnerable. They did send military advisors over to Korea to join up with members of the Japanese legation in Korea to help, but it was insufficient.

In 1882, when King Gojong of Korea heard that his garrison soldiers were underfed due to a famine, he appointed his staff to provide rice. However, corruption came into play by those who wanted him usurped, so the delivery of the rice was contaminated by food agents who used fillers like sand. Consequently, a mutiny came about. It started with attacking the home of Min Gyeom-ho, who they believed was the head conspirator. Gyeom-ho was the overseer of government finances, but he had assigned the matter of distributing the rice to his steward. Gyeom-ho wasn't completely innocent, as he had neglected his duties, but the blame does not rest with him alone.

After this, the massive force then stole ammunition and weapons from the arsenals. A separate group of 3,000 men raced to the Japanese legation, shouting out that they would kill their Japanese guests. Hanabusa Yoshitada, the minister to Korea and the head of the legation, ordered the occupants to evacuate, after which he had the building set on fire. They took refuge at Incheon first until their hosts gained word about what had happened. The Japanese, seeing that their hosts' attitude had changed, fled the city, being pursued by Korean soldiers. Six Japanese were killed, and five were seriously wounded. The survivors were able to board a British ship and escape to safety.

In the end, the Koreans paid reparations to the families of the deceased soldiers, and more money was donated to the Japanese government to help out with the food shortages.

Chinese Meddling in Korea

After the Imo Incident of 1882, China took advantage of Korea's ineffective military response to reassert its own influence in Korean matters. Chinese officers took over the training of the Korean army and provided more advanced weapons and ammunition. China and Korea then signed a treaty, in which Korea would permit itself to be classified as a dependent state of China. A Korean maritime service was created, administered by China, which was a boon to Chinese merchants. Chinese officials were also stationed in various sections of Korea under the rationale that they were protecting Chinese interests.

Both Korea and China were permitted to trade with each other, but China was the country that had a greater advantage as they had more goods.

Japan's Role in the Gapsin Coup

Kim Ok-gyun, a reformist activist, was a Korean who heavily supported the Westernization of Korea and introduced ideas for altering their society to adopt Western sciences, military equipment, and technology. He was also concerned that Japan might invade Korea, and under the guise of learning about new technologies, he went to Japan in 1884. There he discovered that Japan was not imminently planning to attack Korea. Therefore, the Japanese model might be a workable paradigm for Korea, and there wouldn't be any resistance to his explorations in this regard.

Kim also knew that while China's strength was declining, it was simultaneously trying to control Korea to use for its own purposes. Kim supported maintaining the independence of Korea but strongly believed that it would only be possible if reforms were rapidly enacted. Thankfully for him, Kim was a militant activist who was willing to go to the extreme to make that happen.

He and his followers returned to Korea in 1884 and planned a coup d'état to usurp the ultra-conservative King Gojong from his throne. Luckily for them, half of the Chinese soldiers who were present in Korea had been relocated to engage in the skirmishes between France and China over Vietnam. That reduced the number of Chinese forces Kim would have to face before he and his men could carry out the coup d'état. They began their coup at a banquet to celebrate a newly established post office. Kim and his followers approached the king, telling him that the Chinese were creating trouble and that he needed to go with them to a safe place. The group brought King Gojong to a small palace, where he was placed under watch by Japanese legation guards. Several of the Korean government officials who were in attendance at the banquet were either killed or injured.

Following that, Kim set up his fourteen-point reform proposal, which included the abolition of the elite privileges of the ruling class, the establishment of equal rights for all people, the restructure of the government as a constitutional monarchy, the revision of land taxes, the promulgation of free trade and commerce for all, and severe penalties for corruption.

It was a heroic effort, but it was unrealistic in terms of its practicality. The only defenders of the Gaehwapadang, besides the members themselves, were 140 Japanese soldiers from the Japanese legation. And even though half of the Chinese troops had left Korea, they still left a massive amount behind. For instance, the garrison they maintained at Seoul had 1,500 men.

Queen Myeongseong, requested that the Chinese descend upon the rebels, and they did so, killing forty of the Japanese fighters and burning down the Japanese legation building. The activists were then picked up by a Japanese ship. While the weak Japanese ambassador agreed to release them to Korean authorities, the captain of the ship countermanded his order. They were exiled to Japan, with some later moving to the United States. Kim Ok-gyun moved to Japan, living in Tokyo and later Sapporo, and had his name changed to an alias, "Iwata Shusaku." That isn't the end of his story, however.

Although Kim was paranoid about an assassination attempt, he couldn't turn down the chance to travel to Shanghai and meet the noted Chinese politician Li Hongzhang. As he was traveling to meet him, he was shot by a Korean activist. His body was turned over to the Chinese, who dismembered it and carried it through Seoul and several towns. This brutal mutilation triggered the First Sino-Japanese War.

The First Sino-Japanese War July 1894 – August 1895

This war between China and Japan was primarily fought over power in Korea, and the major battles and events are detailed below. It is interesting to note that China was breathing its last in terms of imperial rule. Despite their opposition to Korea and Japan, the last dynasty of China, the Qing dynasty, ended when the Meiji era faded into the sands of time.

Battle of Seonghwan

This was the first land battle of the war, and it took place south of Seoul near the city of Seonghwan, Korea. The Chinese forces were gathered there and had anticipated the arrival of the Japanese, building trenches and earthworks to prepare for the assault. Unfortunately for them, their reinforcements had been lost in an earlier naval battle, and all their supplies and reinforcements had to come by sea via the port of Aswan.

The Japanese, however, realized that most of this war would be fought at sea, as both Korea and Japan are surrounded by water, and the countries involved also had numerous rivers. Japan had been rapidly building a strong navy, and it was clear early on in this war that whichever country could control the water would win the war.

In a demonstration of the fact that the Chinese imperial government often had too much power, Empress Dowager Cixi embezzled some of the money targeted toward updating the Chinese fleets in order to build a sumptuous palace in Beijing. Most of the Chinese vessels were virtual relics; they were bulky and heavy in comparison to the quick-moving Japanese warships.

The primitive naval formation was predictable, as the Chinese warships tended to follow each other as if in a single file. This allowed Japan to form a blockade so that the Chinese garrison in Asan was deprived of reinforcements and fresh provisions.

The battle lasted a day in July of 1894. At the Seoul garrison, the Japanese and Korean land forces overran the Chinese, who were attempting to sequester themselves there. Five hundred of the nearly 4,000 Chinese troops were killed or wounded, and the rest were captured. The Japanese forces which numbered 4,000 suffered less than one hundred casualties.

Battle of Pyongyang

Quickly, China rushed between 13,000 to 15,000 fighters to the Pyongyang garrison. During the dark of night, Japanese warships circled Pyongyang on September 15th, 1894, before attacking on all sides. Three thousand Chinese were killed outright, and 4,000 were injured or missing. If one includes the 102 Japanese who were killed, that means 3,152 men fell within a 24-hour period.

Battle of Pungdo

If a non-combatant vessel was engaged in an act of war, such as aiding the enemy, it was considered to be a justifiable target according to the rules of engagement. At the end of July 1894, two Chinese ships were on their way to meet a British supply ship, the *Kowshing*. One of the Chinese cruisers escaped the attack of the Japanese flying squadron, but the other foundered on the rocks and exploded.

While the Japanese were in the process of guiding the English ship out of the action, the Chinese warriors on board threatened to kill the British captain. Negotiations ensued for four hours until the frustrated Japanese captain fired upon the *Kowshing*. His torpedo missed, but due to the proximity of the two vessels, the merchant ship was broadsided and sunk.

Battle of the Yalu River

On September 17th, 1894, the Japanese fleet met the Chinese Beiyang Fleet near the mouth of the Yalu River, which connects to the Korea Bay. The two most impressive vessels in the Chinese fleet were the *Dingyuan* and the *Zhenyuan*, German-built ironside warships. While they were formidable ships, they ran out of ammunition because they couldn't defeat the smaller, swifter ships of the Japanese navy.

Port Arthur Massacre

Japan had been successfully moving through Korea, and after winning a decisive victory over the Korean city of Pyongyang, they decided to try and capture Port Arthur in China, which was home to the Beiyang Fleet. In November 1894, they had made it to the port, but the Japanese army under General Yamaji Motoharu spotted the mutilated bodies of their fellow soldiers. Their hands and feet had been cut off, while others had been burned alive. This infuriated the troops, and after the city fell to the Japanese, a massacre ensued. A Japanese soldier wrote in his diary that the Japanese were filled with a desire to kill any Chinese soldiers they saw, but they also killed civilians.

> Anyone we saw in the town, we killed. The streets were full of corpses…We killed people in their homes, by and large, there wasn't a single house without three to six dead. Blood was flowing and the smell was awful.

Into Manchuria and Beijing

In January of 1895, the Chinese went into Manchuria, where there was a sheltered harbor at Weihaiwei. However, the Japanese laid siege on Weihaiwei, attacking them both from land and sea for nearly a month. After the fall of Weihaiwei, which was the last major battle fought in the war, the Japanese and Chinese engaged in minor skirmishes, including the Battle of Yinkou.

Although the Chinese sued for peace after the Battle of Weihaiwei, due to the fact that the Japanese could easily capture the capital of Beijing, the Japanese sought to capture Taiwan, making it one of their territories. Instead of attacking the island directly, the Japanese attacked the Pescadores Islands, which were nearby, in late March 1895. It took only three days of fighting for Japan to gain the coveted territory of Taiwan, placing it under Japanese rule until 1945.

Treaty of Shimonoseki, 1895

While the Meiji administration had its own internal problems, it scored a tremendous accomplishment with this war on two levels. First of all, the victory of Japan over the massive mainland country of China remains one of the most important events in its history. Through that victory, Japan proved to the world that it was truly a modern country and merited the respect of being looked upon as totally independent and a force to be reckoned with. Secondly, the territorial gains Japan had made were a boon to the likelihood that future Japanese businesses could become truly international, and

Japan also earned a seat in all the international governmental bodies that dealt with Asian matters.

The most important territories it gained were Taiwan, the Penghu Islands, and the crucial peninsula of Liaodong, which gave it control of the Yellow Sea. Through the treaty, Japan gained the right to use the Yangtze River, and China also recognized the independence of Korea.

Russo-Japanese War (1904 to 1905)

After China's defeat in the Sino-Japanese War in 1895, Japan invaded Manchuria. It was particularly interested in gaining a stronghold with railroads that could access Eurasia. Japan feared that Russia might encroach on its territories, especially since Russia had been leasing Port Arthur, a naval base, from China. To settle the matter, Japan offered to cede control over Manchuria in exchange for Japan having influence over Korea, specifically North Korea. However, Russia refused. The Russian battleships were sheltered at the harbor of Port Arthur, and the Japanese began the war by attacking their fleet in February 1904.

The Battles of Port Arthur and Liaoyang

During the Battle of Port Arthur, one Russian ship was sunk, and two others were badly damaged. The Japanese attempted to blockade the port, so Russia couldn't use it, but two Russian battleships managed to slip out into the open waters. However, they struck Japanese mines, sinking one ship and heavily damaging another. Russia learned from the Japanese and their offense mining, and they also began to place mines in the area, damaging two Japanese ships. The bombardment continued and even moved on to land. Russia sent in reinforcements to protect its fleet, but it wasn't successful, as the Japanese artillery pommeled the moored ships. Every one of Russia's ships was disabled.

The first major land battle of the war was the Battle of Liaoyang, which took place from late August to early September 1904. The city was strategically important to the Russians to maintain a position in southern Manchuria. However, the Russians retreated, making it a Japanese victory, although it should be noted that the Japanese suffered higher casualties than the Russians.

Battle of Tsushima

In May 1905, the Japanese fleet made a punishing trip over the sea to reach the remaining Russian fleet of steel-reinforced battleships. The Japanese ship, *Mikasa*, was constantly hit with Russian gunfire from their ship, *Oslyabya*, and was badly damaged, but the Japanese gunfire prevailed until the Russian flagship sank. The Japanese continued their gunfire and set upon the Russian ship, the *Borodino*, until the ship exploded in a huge fireball. This was followed by the sinking of two more of the Russian battleships.

Nighttime brought torpedo attacks by Japanese submarines and destroyers. The destroyers attacked head-on, while the torpedo boats assaulted the Russian ships from two sides. It was pitch-black, and ships collided with one another. Every time the Russians turned on their searchlights, they revealed their position and were subsequently attacked. Three older Russian cruisers rushed in to help but were hit by torpedoes. The Japanese never relented during the entire night.

At first light, the Japanese fleet chased the Russians northward. The Russians hoisted a facsimile of a surrender flag using tablecloths, as they couldn't locate an actual one. That was deliberate, as Russia insisted its men fight to their deaths. Once the tablecloths were hoisted, they were ignored since they had tried to surrender in several battles during the Sino-Japanese War, and the Japanese now knew that it was a trick. Once the Russians brought their ships to a dead halt, Japan accepted their surrender. This battle was the last major battle of the war, although the peace treaty wasn't concluded until September 1905. The two Russian admirals were faced with charges upon their return home, but the tsar pardoned them from the death penalty. Despite that, the reputations of both men were ruined. Russia had no tolerance for failure, regardless of how justified it might have been.

This battle is notable for being the first decisive naval battle fought with modern steel battleships, and it was also the first naval battle in which the radio played an important role.

Chapter 8 – The Taisho Era

Between 1912 to 1926, Japan continued to modernize. This rapid modernization gobbled up the government's budget, leaving virtually little in reserve. The political situation was made precarious by the death of Emperor Meiji in 1912 and even more so by the cutting of Japan's largest expenditure—the military. Prime Minister Saionji Kinmochi made that decision, and it showed that Japan hadn't yet matured as a sovereign country. As a result of this traumatic change, the army minister resigned, with Kinmochi resigning shortly after. In essence, the country was still learning how to function effectively without looking upon a supreme authority to tell it what to do.

The new emperor, Yoshihito, Meiji's son, took on the imperial name of "Taisho" and responded to this crisis by appointing Katsura Taro as prime minister, who had been the prime minister before Kinmochi. Riots broke out, as Katsura was an elder statesman and the Japanese didn't trust him to propel them into the future. Katsura proved that fact almost immediately by attempting to solve the military crisis by doing the opposite of his predecessor. He restored the military budget but overextended it and virtually ignored the country's focus on its new constitution. In the midst of massive protests and the appointment of Katsura for yet another term, the political parties rose up to resolve the crisis. The Rikken Seiyukai promoted Yamamoto Gonnohyoe as Katsura's replacement, and the emperor approved. That was a mistake.

The Rikken Seiyukai party's interest was in business expansion, and it was later revealed that the Siemens Corporation had conspired to attract more business for itself by obtaining military contracts with the navy and paying a fifteen percent kickback to those who could procure those contracts. The people were furious when they found out, so they looked toward a shakeup of the legislative body, the Diet, to undermine the control of the Rikken Seiyukai and the Siemens Corporation. The scandal led to the collapse of the Yamamoto Cabinet. Hence, the Progressive Party won the majority of positions in the national Diet. Okuma Shigenobu, a leading member of that party, became prime minister in 1914.

Because of the political manipulations that took place from 1912 to 1914, the Japanese navy and military were powerful. When World War I broke out in 1914, Japan seized the opportunity to join the Allied Powers—Russia, France, and the United Kingdom—to subdue the Central Powers of Germany, Austria-Hungary, the Ottoman Empire, and Bulgaria from gaining control over the rich sea lanes in the Pacific Ocean. Japan's hidden agenda in creating agreements with the Allies was to expand its influence on China, whose international commerce depended upon the Pacific.

Japan in World War I

At the end of July 1914 and the beginning of August of the same year, the Allied Powers in Europe came together against Germany and Austria-Hungary over control in Europe. In order for the Allies to be successful, though, Germany needed to be weakened.

Germany had a number of colonies in the Pacific which their navy had to protect—the German colony of Qingdao on the Chinese mainland, the Marshall Islands, Papua New Guinea, the Solomon Islands, the Northern Mariana Islands, Samoa, and the smaller island chains of Micronesia in the South Pacific. It was tantamount to a mini-empire in the East.

The Allies were interested in eliminating the power of the Imperial German Navy in the Far East, and Great Britain, in particular, urged Japan to manage that area of the war. In the name of Emperor Taisho, Japan declared war on Germany.

Japan's first target was the German colony of Qingdao. Japan surrounded Qingdao and put it under siege. Several months later, Germany surrendered control of that colony. While in this area, Japan attacked Shandong Province via Jiaozhou Bay. That bay led out to the Yellow Sea, which Japan had coveted control over for years.

Docked in Jiaozhou Bay were an Austria-Hungarian sea cruiser, the SMS *Kaiserin Elisabeth*, and a German gunboat. Japanese efforts to evict them from the area were initially unsuccessful. With the aid of the British forces, though, it was overrun and occupied by both Britain and Japan.

The Japanese navy went on to seize the Mariana Islands and the Marshall Islands. There was no resistance on the part of the Germans, who were overwhelmed with events in the European theater of the war.

Twenty-One Demands

In early January 1915, Prime Minister Shigenobu and Foreign Minister Kato Takaaki presented 21 demands to China divided into 5 groups: 1) confirmation of Japanese control over Shandong Province, along with its railways and the Chinese coast along there; 2) exclusive ownership of a section of southern Manchuria and access to the raw materials in Inner Mongolia; 3) Japanese control over a metallurgical complex in central China; 4) a prohibition on China to allow foreign countries to have concessions to the Chinese coast and its islands; and 5) Japan could have advisors in China who could take over their finances and its police. Demand five was kept secret until absolutely necessary because it would essentially make China subservient to Japan.

After discussions with China, Japan reduced the number of demands to thirteen. Fearing war with Japan, China conceded to the revised demands and signed a treaty with Japan in late May 1915.

Although Japan and China made peace regarding the Chinese mainland, there were more issues that were left unsettled. In 1916, Great Britain indicated that they would support Japanese claims to the German colonies in the Pacific if Japan was willing to use their navy to assist with the ongoing war in the Western Hemisphere by escorting British battleships and performing rescues in the Mediterranean.

The United States entered the war and joined the Allies in 1917, although they were not officially an ally, instead preferring to be an "associated power" to avoid future wars. They knew of Japan's interest in controlling the Pacific and wanted that modified, but the needs of the Allies superseded that interest, at least until the end of the war.

In 1917, Japan's second squadron escorted and defended British transport vessels and provided manpower to aid in the anti-submarine warfare in the Mediterranean Sea. They also provided invaluable rescues at sea, including that of 3,000 people from an American ship, the SS *Transylvania*, which was transporting troops to the front lines.

The British were very pleased with the rapidity of Japan's response to sudden requests and crises on the seas due to warfare. France was also appreciative of the fact that Japan was able to secure twelve destroyers for its use in the war. Due to its modernization efforts, Japanese businesses and its military were experienced in import-export operations, and that impressed the other Allied countries. Japan was also experienced in obtaining war materials and provisions for the troops. They benefited a lot during this war, as they learned a lot of military techniques and absorbed some new technologies from Europe.

In 1917, the Bolshevik Revolution occurred in Russia, and Japan sent troops there in 1918 along with the United States. They were ordered to go to the harsh cold area of Siberia in order to strengthen the armies of Admiral Alexander Kolchak, who was waging a war against the Bolsheviks who were attempting to control much of the territory there. One of the reasons for the US entering the war was to halt the spread of communism. That was the brainchild of the Bolshevik Revolution essentially, but it did serve the purpose of helping to put an end to World War I. War weariness crept in as the war threatened to spread from country to country. Already the Ottomans and the Turks in the Middle East were fighting. In Russia, the struggle between the White Army and the Red Army of the Bolsheviks was a civil war. Austria-Hungary was dealing with dwindling resources to keep up the fight. The only reason Japan was involved was to aid in the Siberian front to aid the Americans. Later, in 1922, Tsarist Russia fell, and the Bolsheviks prevailed.

Treaty of Versailles

As a result of Japan's contribution toward the victory of the Allied Powers, Japan joined up with the "Big Four." The Big Four refers to the four major powers of the Allies who were at the peace conference to draw up the treaty. Japan was later included in that circle.

The Treaty of Versailles granted Japan the right to administer the islands they had conquered at the beginning of the war. Japan also received rights to Jiaozhou Bay, which would finally give Japan access to the Yellow Sea. The German-owned islands south of the Pacific were awarded to Australia, meaning that Micronesia, formerly controlled by Germany, was now on the path toward becoming independent.

United States President Woodrow Wilson supported Japan's right to administer the islands north of the equator that they had annexed during the war. However, that didn't mean that Japan owned those islands. They controlled them under the mandates of the newly formed League of Nations, which was intended to resolve disputes among countries and avoid future wars.

Japan was also allowed to maintain their control over Shandong Province in China, which they annexed during the war. Later on, in 1919, a fierce dispute over Japan's annexation of the Chinese province of Shandong arose. China wouldn't sign the treaty if Japan was allowed to control that province, and the matter wasn't resolved until 1922. Japan, unfortunately, had to give up its right to Shandong; however, it was still permitted to retain economic control of the railway there.

Japan proposed a "racial equality clause" to the Treaty of Versailles. Japan wanted to be treated as equals, and although their proposal was considered to be for universal racial equality, Japan just wanted it for those members of the League of Nations, of which it was a founding member. The Japanese knew they had been forced to sign unequal treaties after Matthew Perry opened the door for the rest of the world to enter Japan, and they wanted to prevent that from happening. But the idea of universal racial equality, which was what most of the peace conference assumed Japan wanted, was not really possible at the time, mostly due to the Western powers seeking more and more domains of non-white people to add to their empire.

Through several machinations, it was determined that a unanimous vote was needed to pass it. The United States, the United Kingdom, Portugal, and Romania didn't vote for the inclusion of the racial equality proposal, and as a result, Japan was inclined toward not cooperating with the Western nations.

The issues arising from the exclusion of the racial equality proposal weren't resolved until after World War II.

Effects of World War I on Japan

Prosperity descended upon Japan after the war. The corporate conglomerates and the *zaibatsu* organized during the Meiji era expanded during the Taisho era. The Allied Powers' need for military provisions, the use of ships from the Japanese navy, Japan's facility in the import-export business, and their banking sector created a boom in their economy. Later on, Japan became a creditor nation because of its dependence on imports. Japan even made agreements with Taiwan and Korea to grow rice.

Inflation was one of the fallouts of the war. Wages hadn't kept pace with the rising prices, which caused the Rice Riots of 1918. This didn't only affect the poor, as middle-income families also struggled with the rising prices. Because of the disparities in social classes, it encouraged the founding of the Japanese Communist Party in 1922. Socialism was attractive as it was felt that it would provide a solution to the many problems the lower classes faced. The Japanese Communist Party, though, had distinct differences from the Bolsheviks, as it didn't rest upon violent revolutions as a means of control.

After World War I, Japanese troops continued fighting in Siberia until 1922. The country was concerned about the anti-monarchical stance of the Bolshevik regime in Russia, as that contradicted Japan's governmental structure. Furthermore, many felt that communists might infiltrate Japan's government. Japan had gone through a painful period in order to convert to a constitutional monarchy and couldn't withstand another major change. Japan lost about 5,000 men in the Siberian expedition and lost the battle to oust the Bolsheviks. What's more, it suffered a large economic loss financing the Siberian effort. Not only were there the expenditures of conducting warfare, but Japanese banks made loans to Russia for the Siberian expedition, which Russia defaulted on. The Siberian expedition also contributed in part to creating a shortage of rice because the government had to buy it for their troops.

The other factor that created the food shortage during this period was the Great Kanto earthquake in 1923.

Great Kanto Earthquake

The epicenter of this earthquake was near Tokyo, in the heart of Japan. It registered at 7.9 on the moment magnitude scale (the successor of the Richter scale) and is one of the most powerful earthquakes that Japan has ever experienced. Widespread damage spread over the capital city and the surrounding cities and towns, including Yokohama, a nearby port. Over 140,000 people died, and since the earthquake occurred during lunchtime, when fires were being used to cook food, some of those deaths were due to fires being spread throughout the city. The single greatest loss of life actually occurred due to the fires when 38,000 people lost their lives after taking shelter in a clothing store. The earthquake also triggered landslides and a tsunami, which devasted the homes and lives of the people. A rumor arose that the Koreans who were living in Japan at the time were taking advantage of the disaster, that they were looting and committing arson. As a result, a countless number of Koreans were killed by mobs, with some estimating the number to be between 6,000 and 10,000.

The government placed the Koreans into protective custody, and martial law was declared. Despite that, the rumor grew to implicate socialists. Historians indicate that this was a move fostered by the imperial government to rid the country of political dissidents.

As a result of the earthquake, Tokyo underwent reconstruction. This was a backhanded opportunity to replace poorly constructed buildings up to standard. Of course, the recovery was very costly.

Universal Male Suffrage

The rise of democracy in Japan was strong during the Taisho era. There were demonstrations regarding the requirement that voter eligibility depended upon income. Because of that, it was difficult for the general public to run their own candidates through the political parties. The government, therefore, was run by the few, even in the 1920s. That fact alone reminded the people of old Japan that the emperor and his advisors dictated policies to the working public. The pro-business political party, the Rikken Seiyukai, was extremely powerful, so smaller political parties experienced slow growth. They were often unable to get candidates elected who represented the rural interests and those of medium-level wage earners.

Gradually, a new Kenseito political party emerged upon the ashes of the old Kenseito Party, which had collapsed during the Meiji era. The Kenseito party proposed the General Election Law in 1925, and it was passed by the Diet. This law stated that all males 25 years of age and older were allowed to vote, regardless of income.

Women weren't allowed to attend political meetings until 1922, so they did not achieve the right to vote at this time. The women's suffrage movement continued to grow, though, and women finally were given the right to vote in 1945.

Chapter 9 – The Showa Era

Hirohito succeeded Emperor Taisho in 1926, taking the title Emperor Showa. In the West, emperors from this point onward are more often remembered for their birth names than their name as emperor, which is how they are referred to after they die in Japan (while they are alive, they go by "His Majesty" or "His Majesty the Emperor") so they will be referred to as such in this book. The Showa era lasted until Hirohito's death in 1989.

There was a financial crisis following World War I due to all of the expenditures associated with the war and the very rapid democratization movements taking place within the country.

The Naval Race

After noting the necessity of having vibrant navies, the major powers who participated in World War I engaged in vigorous shipbuilding. The mad pace of the construction of warships and aircraft carriers was alarming. The ultimate purpose of this was the control of the Pacific Ocean. America, Great Britain, and Japan all had competing interests there. Returning to some sense of rationality after this initial frenzy, these nations discussed limitations. In 1922, the issue was discussed and continued to be discussed by nine of the nations involved in World War I, at what was called the Washington Naval

Conference, but no agreement was reached with regard to ships other than battleships and carriers. All the countries, however, recognized the importance of balancing its naval programs.

Other treaties were introduced within the next decade or so, which sought additional limitations on the construction of battleships. The terms of the original 1922 treaty were modified by the London Naval Treaty of 1930 and then the Second London Naval Treaty of 1936. However, Japan did not sign the Second London Naval Treaty. They saw the limitations of how many ships they could have in their navy as another snub by the United States, which only added to the tensions between the two countries. By the end of December 1934, the Japanese government had given formal notice that it intended to terminate the naval treaties it was engaged with.

The Manchurian Incident

The National Policy Company of Japan, whose function was to operate railways in northeastern China, acquired the south Manchurian railroad in 1906. To guard Japanese interests, a division of the Japanese army called the Kwantung Army was stationed there. After World War I, the Chinese built their own railroad, which ran parallel to the south Manchurian one. To eliminate this competition and help Japan gain stronger control over China, the Kwantung Army blew up a section of their own tracks in 1931. They did that so they could blame the explosion on the Chinese and create a pretext for invading Manchuria.

The Japanese troops then clashed with the Chinese soldiers and forced them north into northern China. By 1932, the Kwantung Army controlled all of Manchuria, setting up a puppet state called Manchukuo. The general of the Kwantung Army placed himself in the role of ambassador. All of this was done without any permission from the central government, and Tokyo reluctantly accepted the Manchukuo state, as it had already been done.

Realizing the implications of permitting this branch of the Japanese army to gain control over Japan, Prime Minister Inukai Tsuyoshi attempted to restrain the Kwantung Army before being assassinated by rebels in the Japanese navy who wanted the military to control the government. The plot, known as the May 15 Incident, also included attacking other prominent politicians and even assassinating the famous film star Charlie Chaplin to incite tension with the United States; however, Chaplin was watching a sumo match with the prime minister's son and was able to escape.

Rise of the Right

After the prime minister was assassinated, more young radicals vehemently opposed any reduction in military spending and attempted a coup d'état in 1936 under the leadership of Shumei Okawa. Since Emperor Hirohito stood on the right politically, he resented the fact that these young leftist radicals were trying to manipulate him. He responded by quashing the coup and arresting the perpetrators. Some were executed, including Ikki Kita, a noted socialist who opposed imperial domination.

In 1936, the liberals assassinated Takahashi Korekiyo, a rather conservative member of the House of Peers. Takahashi was one of the politicians who supported a cut in military spending, as he was a member of the Rikken Seiyukai party, which backed the economic and burgeoning business interests of Japan.

Japan was then on the road toward autocratic rule. The Diet approved of unilateral military interventions and expansionism with the objective of establishing a Japanese empire. Political parties and clubs that promulgated this ideology proliferated, including the Imperial Way Society, the National Foundation Party, the Society for the Preservation of the National Essence, and the National Purity Society.

The Second Sino-Japanese War

Fortified by their conquest of Manchuria in 1931, Japan aggressively pursued all the rights it felt it deserved after World War I. Its leadership was clamoring for control of China without any concessions, as well as southeast Asia so as to set up the "Empire of

Japan." The Chinese, in particular, wanted to maintain the sovereignty of their own country—control they had held onto for centuries. By virtue of the Treaty of Versailles, Japan had to surrender control of Shandong Province, which they occupied during the war. They resented that and considered the agreement forged at Versailles to be an unequal treaty.

Not only had Japan annexed Manchuria, but they also obtained the rights to the raw materials in Inner Mongolia during the Taisho era. On the other hand, Chiang Kai-shek, the chairman of the National Government of the Republic of China, spent his efforts attempting to develop the ideals of a nationalist China. He was opposed to the communists who advocated a united front against the Japanese. In view of the fact that he opposed Japan, Chiang Kai-shek tried to drive out Japanese influence from China. That exploded into the Second Sino-Japanese War, which melded into World War II.

It all started in 1937 when Japan gained control of the Marco Polo Bridge, which led to the main route into Beijing. In retaliation, Chiang Kai-shek had his forces place a siege upon the Shanghai International Settlement, which was a territory composed of British and American civilians. Although some have called the subsequent bombing accidental, the result was the same. Three thousand Japanese civilians were killed, and after that, the Chinese army attacked the Japanese navy stationed near Shanghai.

The Battle of Shanghai

After the destruction at the Shanghai International Settlement, Chinese aircraft bombarded Japanese ships in and near the harbor in 1937. Although the Chinese pilots waged a ferocious battle in the air over Shanghai, the Japanese were able to hold on to their defensive positions for a while, as the Chinese suffered heavy casualties in the face of the more experienced Japanese. After Japanese troops captured the Dachang district within Shanghai, the National Revolutionary Army of China was forced to retreat.

Japan initially wanted to stop the war early on and discuss terms, but its victory at Shanghai wetted Japan's interest in continuing, so further attacks were authorized.

The Battle of Nanking

In 1937, Nanking was the capital of China. After it conquered Shanghai, Japan then marched on this city. General Iwane Matsui counterattacked, and for two days, the two sides fought. However, Chiang Kai-shek abandoned the defense of Nanking, as his forces couldn't hold out because they were outnumbered two to one. Many of the Chinese soldiers shed their uniforms and disappeared into the non-combatant population.

Inflated by their victory, the Japanese army executed Chinese prisoners of war, massacred the civilian population, raped women, and looted stores and homes. This caused an international outcry and became known as the Nanking Massacre.

Battle of Wuhan

In 1938, Chiang Kai-shek had to move the capital from the conquered city of Nanking to Wuhan. The Yangtze and Han Rivers divide the city into three regions—Hankou, Hanyang, and Wuchang. Hankou was the commercial region, Hanyang was the industrial district, and Wuchang housed the government. The Japanese forces followed Chiang Kai-shek, who wanted to defend the railway stationed in Wuhan and have accommodations for his administrative offices. China placed a huge number of troops there, close to 800,000. The Chinese stubbornly defended the area against the Kwantung Army, so Japan—in desperation—launched a poison gas attack and then seized Wuhan.

The fighting continued into 1939, and the Japanese gained Wuhan, but their victory came at a high cost; it is estimated that 1.2 million casualties occurred with both sides combined. The offensive left the Japanese fairly weakened, and the battle only bought the Chinese extra time to move their forces and equipment farther inland, making this a tactical victory for the Japanese but a strategic one for the Chinese.

Battle of Suixian-Zaoyang

In April 1939, the Chinese army had their 77th Division defending this southeastern territory because of the Japanese harbor blockades. The Chinese were attempting to prevent Japan from landing there and moving inland. Of course, the Chinese were more familiar with the terrain, which was very mountainous, and Japan lost the battle in late May. This appeared to be a turning point in the war, as it invigorated the Chinese army who were inspired to continue resisting, hoping that this would become a war of attrition.

Battle of Kunlun Pass

In 1939, the Chinese had been receiving military provisions through French Indochina via the mountainous Kunlun Pass. Japan, who already had limited control of Kunlun, wanted to cut off any more shipments to China. The newly formed 200th Division of the Chinese Revolutionary Army was a vicious and determined fighting force. Under the guidance of Brigade Commander Dai Anlan, the Chinese were able to split up the defending Japanese ground forces at the pass early in 1940, killing Japanese Major General Masao Nakamura in the process. The Japanese could only rely upon their air power at this point, but they were unable to prevail. Hence, the Chinese successfully regained control of the Kunlun Pass.

After that, China moved is capital to Chungking. Chiang Kai-shek then kept moving his army westward toward the Yangtze River and continued presenting a fierce resistance. In 1938, General Iwane Matsui of China received a message that he was going to be relieved of his command, along with eight other members of his senior staff, so there was a shakeup of the command structure.

From 1939 to 1942, Japan attempted to blockade the Chinese ports along the coast.

The Tientsin Incident

In 1939, the Japanese army blockaded foreign concessions in the Chinese port of Tientsin because the British took custody of four Chinese men who killed a Japanese official. When Japan requested that they be handed over to the Japanese authorities, the British refused. The Japanese responded by outrageously demanding the silver reserves held in British banks; they also strip-searched anyone leaving the port and blocked the importation of food and fuel.

In view of the fact that this would accelerate and widen the war. Britain remanded the Chinese into Japan's custody, and they were summarily executed.

Battle of South Henan

In early 1941, the Japanese clashed with the Chinese Revolutionary Army in the province of Henan. The Japanese split their army into three divisions in order to attack the Chinese. However, the Chinese avoided full-frontal assaults and spread out their forces to coax the Japanese into thinning out into a line. The Chinese then maneuvered in such a way that they were able to outflank the Japanese and squeeze them like a vice. Before that move could occur, the Japanese withdrew, and the Chinese was still able to maintain control of Henan.

American Interference

Starting in the year 1938, America extended loans to China upon hearing about the deaths of unarmed Chinese civilians. In addition, the US was aware of the inferior military position of China and began providing China with arms and ammunition. Furthermore, the US objected to Japan's use of its manufactured military products, like airplanes, ammunition, and even oil for their ships and aircraft. Aside from some moral embargoes, which forbade the shipment of war materials to Imperial Japan, America didn't want to become too involved in the conflict in the Pacific. Since the US vehemently protested aggressive actions against China by Japan, the American and Japanese positions became irreconcilable. The US secretary of state, Cordell Hull, strove for an agreement between China and

Japan, calling for the withdrawal of Japan from China, the recognition of the sovereign leadership of Chiang Kai-shek, and a non-aggression policy between Japan and the islands in the Pacific Ocean.

An imperial conference was held in Tokyo, and it was decided that the American solution was unacceptable. In 1941, Minister of War Hideki Tojo was appointed as prime minister and loudly advocated the expansionist policies of Japan in the Pacific. In November of the same year, Admiral Isoroku Yamamoto, who was actually strongly against the war in China to the point of receiving death threats, ordered an attack on the American naval fleet at Pearl Harbor, Hawaii, in order to preemptively strike against the US in the inevitable war between the two countries.

Cordell Hull sensed that there might be a Japanese attack on American battle cruisers but thought it would occur in the Philippines or Malaya. However, that was not to be the case. Early on the morning of December 7th, 1941, Japanese aircraft were launched to attack the naval base of Pearl Harbor. As a result, 188 American airplanes were obliterated, all eight battleships were damaged, with four of them sinking, and 2,403 Americans, both soldiers and civilians, were killed, with 1,178 being wounded. The Japanese losses were light in comparison with 29 aircraft being destroyed and 64 men being killed in action. It was an undeniable tragedy in the annals of American history, but it was a major victory for the Japanese, who announced war on the United States that same day.

Chapter 10 – Japan in World War II and Its Aftermath

Although the Japanese declared war that day, the message wasn't delivered until the next day, the same day Franklin Delano Roosevelt delivered his *Infamy Speech* and the US Congress declared war on Japan. Three days later, Benito Mussolini, the dictator of Italy, and Adolph Hitler, the leader of Nazi Germany, declared war on the United States. The United States then joined the European Allies—the United Kingdom, France, the Soviet Union, China, Australia, Canada, South Africa, among others, to fight in the European theater of the war, as well as the Pacific theater. Japan had joined up with what was called the Axis Powers—Germany and Italy, along with other less powerful countries—when they signed the Tripartite Pact with them in September 1940.

The Philippines Campaign

Nine hours after the attack on Pearl Harbor, Japan targeted the Philippine Islands. Japan launched its invasion from Taiwan, which they controlled at the time. The Allied defenders on the islands were members of the Philippine National Guard and other miscellaneous troops who hadn't expected to be involved in any decisive action in World War II. Even though their arrival was a total surprise, the

American-Filipino forces managed to last until April, but guerilla resistance still continued against the Japanese occupants after that.

The Malayan and Dutch East Indies Campaigns

Since these islands were so close together, the losses inflicted on one territory affected the other. An hour before the attack on Pearl Harbor, the Japanese landed on Malaysia, battling with the British Indian Army that was located there. The airport located in Kota Bharu, where the fighting was taking place, was captured, followed by more airports being captured the following day. The British failed to reinforce their dwindling troops throughout this campaign, and coupled with the monsoon season, they were no match for the Japanese, who cleverly used bicycles to work their way through the heavy jungle terrain. They were able to push the British, Indians, and Australians back, winning battle after battle. By the end of January, all of Malaysia was in the hands of the Japanese.

On December 17th, 1941, the Japanese planned to attack Borneo, landing in Malaysia to begin their airstrikes on the island. After gaining some important areas in Borneo, they next decided to capture the oil resources in the East Indies, which would cripple the Allied war efforts in the Pacific. Since the ABDA (American-British-Dutch-Australian Command) had differing views on what was most important to protect, they were unable to stop the progression of the Japanese, who also held much larger numbers than they did. Although ABDA put up fierce resistance against the Japanese, the Japanese had managed to gain many airports in the Dutch East Indies and had decimated their naval forces by late February. On March 9th, the Dutch surrendered.

Battle of Hong Kong

On the morning of December 8th, 1941, Japan attacked the British colony of Hong Kong. There was a huge garrison there, with Chinese, British, and Canadian units occupying. The battle spread out from the garrison into many neighboring areas, and despite a large number of Allied troops, the Japanese forces outnumbered them significantly. This engagement lasted for nearly a month, but the Allied forces had to abandon Hong Kong, leaving it in the hands of the Japanese.

The Burma Campaign

In January of 1942, Japan invaded the country of Burma, mainly because of the Burma Road, which was a major supply route to China, and its control would cut China off from badly needed supplies. Burma also had minerals and a lot of rice, which could serve to feed the Japanese troops for the duration of the war. To bolster its potential success, Japan recruited many Burmese and recruits from the country of Thailand. Thailand and Japan actually created an agreement between them, and the Thai assumed much of the responsibility for conducting the battle.

The Allied forces—Great Britain, the United States, and China—briefly held on to the capital city of Rangoon, but they were forced back by the hardy Japanese. In the craziness, thousands of Burmese citizens were attempting to escape the country. The government was progressively unable to organize in the confusion and evacuate the civilians. The Japanese took this opportunity to successfully defeat the Chinese troops as they were trying to flee to India. With the aid of US Lieutenant General Joseph Stilwell, the chaotic Chinese were reorganized and returned for a counterattack. However, many of them died attempting to pass through a mountainous region. Although the British and American allies outnumbered the Japanese, they were poorly trained, and nearly 31,000 of them died.

The battle trolled on throughout the region and resulted in the Japanese occupation of Burma, although military actions occurred and reoccurred whenever the Americans and the British renewed their attacks. Because of its strategic role, the Allied forces never gave up in their attempt to control Burma. In 1943, Lord Louis Mountbatten took over the Allied command and placed Field Marshal William Slim on the ground. Instead of employing guerilla techniques that the British had used earlier in the campaign, they now had air support. That gave the Allied forces access to supplies, and they also didn't have to use strike-and-run tactics. Once that occurred, the Allies were now fighting on open northern land instead of the jungles, which allowed them to gain ground. Then, in 1945, the second-largest city, Mandalay, fell into Allied hands. The Allies crossed the Irrawaddy River and took Rangoon. Pockets of Japanese continued to struggle, attempting to escape into Thailand. However, Thailand had the support of pro-Allied rebels, which prevented the entrenchment of the Japanese. In July 1945, a few months before the war ended, the Allies occupied Burma.

Battle of Singapore

Between February 8th and 15th, 1942, the Japanese empire attacked the British military base in Singapore. This was a sizeable naval base, and it was considered to be the key to British success in the Pacific war theater. The Allies had already suffered severe losses from the previous campaigns, in particular, the Malayan one, but attempted to put up a fierce fight. However, they were no match for the Japanese. It was a major loss for the Allies, and the largest British surrender in history, with 80,000 British, Indian, and Australian troops becoming prisoners of war (along with the 50,000 taken during the Malayan Campaign). Not only that, but their battleships were decimated or sunk by the proficient Japanese navy.

Battle of the Coral Sea

At the beginning of May in 1942, Japan sought to establish a southern base from which to gain control of the South Pacific, coveting Port Moresby on the southern coast of New Guinea in particular. All the fighting was conducted by aircraft carriers at sea and included Australian participation. Both sides claimed to be victorious in this battle, as the Japanese won a tactical victory by sinking several US ships, including *Lexington*, which represented a good chunk of the US carrier strength in the Pacific. However, the Japanese failed to seize control of the port, which would have been a strategically located southerly anchor point in the Pacific. This was also the first time the Japanese invading force was turned back from their objective, which greatly boosted the morale of the Allies.

Battle of Midway

Midway is an island that lies northwest of Hawaii. In early June of 1942, Admiral Isoroku Yamamoto and his fleet sailed from the Aleutian Islands off Alaska (then known as the Alaska Territory) and attacked what he predicted to be the remaining functioning American ships in the area. However, US Admiral Chester Nimitz was in possession of the decryption codes for Japanese transmissions and was prepared. He attacked the Japanese ships from the land and from aircraft carriers, crippling them. Japan lost four of its aircraft carriers and retreated.

The Guadalcanal Campaign

It was now August of 1942. Not having gained its coveted position in the South Pacific, Japan needed to find something else that would be suitable. Because supplies were being pumped to the Allies in the Pacific by Australia, Japan was in the process of constructing an airbase in the northern area of the Solomon Islands off the coast of New Guinea. Those islands are located northeast of New Guinea and are filled with dense jungles. That geographical factor enabled the two sides to hide their activities. In fact, many of the islanders who lived there weren't aware of them, particularly of the Japanese base. The Japanese ships near New Guinea and the Solomon Islands shipped supplies and materials to the island of Guadalcanal and the surrounding South Pacific area stealthily at night via a route dubbed the "Tokyo Express."

The Allies were determined to prevent Japan from using its base at Guadalcanal to disrupt the Americans from staging operations in the South Pacific. They then launched an offensive attack and managed to seize control of the base, which they called Henderson Field. Admiral Isoroku Yamamoto had 1,400 soldiers and 500 seamen, whom he ordered to retake the base. In addition, Japan had warships in position along with a formidable carrier force. Ground and air attacks ensued, and the sea was filled with torpedoes and smoke from the bombing of the ships. One of the Japanese carriers, the *Ryujo*, was sunk by the end of August. The other two Japanese carriers, the *Shokaku* and the *Zuikaku*, though, weren't damaged. America had two carriers, the USS *Saratoga* and the USS *Enterprise*.

In October of 1942, the Japanese land troops tried to take Henderson Field. They conducted naval and ground attacks before sending out airplanes. The bombardment continued until the airfield was destroyed, but Japan didn't capture it. As soon as the haze cleared, the Americans initiated repairs and called for replacements of planes and ships.

In November, the Japanese attempted to take the airbase again. However, US aircraft saw the approach of Vice-Admiral Hiroaki Abe's force and alerted the Allies. Early on the morning of November 13th, 1942, US Rear Admiral Daniel Callaghan and his force intercepted Abe's force. In the dark, the two warship forces opened fire on each other, making the battle very chaotic. Abe managed to sink or seriously damage all but one cruiser and one destroyer in Callaghan's fleet. Callaghan also died in the battle, along with US Rear Admiral Norman Scott.

Although the Allies lost the battle, they did manage to inflict damage on the Japanese forces. Two Japanese destroyers were sunk, and the *Hiei*, a battleship, was severely damaged; the *Hiei* actually sunk later that day. Due to this destruction of his force, Abe ordered his men to retreat.

On the following day, November 14th, Vice-Admiral Gunichi Mikawa oversaw a cruiser and destroyer force that was sent to attack Henderson Field. They caused some damage, but they weren't incredibly successful in their endeavors. As they retreated, Rear Admiral Raizo Tanaka, believing that Henderson Field was now inoperable, began to head toward Guadalcanal. Throughout the day, aircraft from Henderson Field and the *Enterprise*, a US carrier, attacked the forces of both Mikawa and Tanaka, and they managed to sink one heavy cruiser and seven of the Japanese transports.

Tanaka continued his run toward Guadalcanal, and Admiral Nobutake Kondo began to approach Henderson Field to begin his bombardment of it. Admiral William Halsey Jr. sent out the *Washington* and the *South Dakota*, two US battleships, along with four destroyers to take down Kondo's force. Kondo made quick work of the Allied fleet, sinking three of the destroyers and damaging the fourth one. As they were concentrated on attacking the *South Dakota*, the *Washington* managed to sneak up behind and opened fire on the *Kirishima*, a Japanese battleship, causing major damage to it.

Kondo ordered a retreat, and four Japanese transports beached on Guadalcanal and tried to unload equipment. Shortly after, American air and ground support destroyed the equipment. There were still some Japanese troops on Guadalcanal, but shipments of food and supplies for them via the Tokyo Express were insufficient for the Japanese stranded there. Many died of malnutrition and disease. Finally, by December 12th, Japan abandoned any efforts to retake Guadalcanal.

Allied Air Raids on Japan

In the middle of 1944, the Allied forces—America, Great Britain, and China—decided to attack Japan itself. American B-24 "Liberator" bombers and B-29 "Superfortress" bombers flew out of the Mariana Islands, which lay to the southeast of Japan. There were bombing raids on the city of Osaka in March, June, and August. A total of over 1,700 bombs were dropped, and the city lay in ruins. In March of 1945, in Kobe, civilian targets were bombed, giving rise to severe accusations based on ethical reasons. In June of 1945, bombers attacked Fukuoka, destroying almost one-quarter of the city.

Battle of Okinawa

Okinawa is one of the islands in the Kyushu area of Japan located south of the country, just 300 miles north of Taiwan. The Battle of Okinawa began with an amphibious attack by the United States in early April 1945 in order to gain the airbase there to begin Operation Downfall, which would have the Allies invading the islands of Japan. The battle didn't end until late June, meaning that the war in Europe had already ended by the middle of this campaign since Germany surrendered in May.

This battle was an incredibly fierce fight between the two sides. Japan employed kamikaze pilots for ferocious attacks designed to destroy large areas and enemy equipment by slamming an aircraft loaded with bombs straight into the targets. That resulted in the death of the pilots as well, but they were fully prepared to make that sacrifice. There were huge numbers of Allied tanks on Okinawa that pounded the Japanese defenses for almost three months, not to mention the ships that surrounded the island. Due to the intense fighting, this was one of the bloodiest battles of the war, with around 160,000 casualties from both sides.

Perhaps one of the greatest tragedies of this battle was the loss of civilian life. Estimates indicate that around 300,000 civilians lived on the island, and by the end of the war, between one-tenth and one-third of them had died. Part of the reason was due to the Americans finding it difficult, or just didn't care enough, to distinguish between civilians and soldiers. One soldier reported, "There was some return fire from a few of the houses, but the others were probably occupied by civilians and we didn't care...Americans always had great compassion, especially for children (but) now we fired indiscriminately." Nevertheless, the Japanese also showed indifference toward civilians, often using them as shields, confiscating their food, and murdering those who hid food or who they thought could be spies. Many were killed by starvation and malaria, and others even killed themselves after the Japanese forces, knowing that their defeat was imminent, told them that the Americans would kill and rape them, as many believed in the stereotype that the Americans were barbarians who would actually commit such crimes.

The annexation of Okinawa was originally intended to provide a place from which a full-scale ground and air invasion of the island of Japan could be launched. However, that strategy was scrapped in favor of a plan to use two atomic bombs on Nagasaki and Hiroshima. The Allies contacted Emperor Hirohito of Japan and demanded their full and unconditional surrender, or else Japan would face "utter destruction." The emperor refused, and the plan went ahead.

Atomic Bombings of Nagasaki and Hiroshima

On August 6th and August 9th, 1945, the bombs were dropped on Nagasaki and Hiroshima by US forces. Between 70,000 and 80,000 people died in Hiroshima by the blast and the resultant firestorm. Since Japan showed no indication of surrendering after US President Harry Truman once again asked for it, the Allies agreed to drop the other bomb on Nagasaki, with 25,000 to 75,000 immediately dying. For months and years afterward, though, people continued to die from radiation illness and related injuries, with starvation also occurring. Over the next two to four months, it has been estimated that between 90,000 and 146,000 people in Hiroshima had died, with the estimates for Nagasaki being between 39,000 and 80,000.

The Kyujo Incident: A Coup?

On August 12th, 1945, Major General Kenji Hatanaka, Lieutenant Colonels Ida Masataka, Masahiko Takeshita, and Masao Inada approached the war minister, Korechika Anami, asking that he prevent any attempts at surrender. Anami was the most important man in Japan next to the emperor himself, but he refused and indicated that he planned to ask Emperor Hirohito to record the announcement that Japan would surrender unconditionally to the Allies.

Many of the military commanders felt that Japan should continue to resist the Allies. They were convinced that the Japanese would be enslaved by the Allied forces, although the preliminary agreements specified no such thing. The emperor made the recording of the surrender to be broadcast and put it in the hands of the commanders of the Imperial Guards, Lieutenant General Takeshi Mori and General Shizuichi Tanaka.

Kenji Hatanaka, a military officer, decided to put in motion a plan to stop the surrender from happening. He and a group of men managed to convince Colonel Toyojiro Haga to join their cause, although he only did so by lying to him. Hatanaka told Haga that the commanders of the Eastern District Army and the Imperial Guards Division were all in on the plan. He hoped that just by being inside the palace, others in the army would be inspired to join in and continue the war.

Once inside, Hatanaka shot and killed Lieutenant General Takeshi Mori, as he refused to join the rebels. Hatanaka also murdered Mori's brother-in-law, Michinori Shiraishi, who was in a meeting with Mori when Hatanaka and his forces barged in. Hatanaka then had his rebels cut the communication lines to the outside world.

At around the same time, another group of rebels went to kill Prime Minister Kantaro Suzuki. However, Suzuki had already been warned, so the building was empty. The rebels elected to burn it down and then headed to Kiichiro Hiranuma's, the former prime minister, house to kill him instead. He managed to escape, although his house was burned down.

Hatanaka's plot began to unravel around him, and he was informed that the Eastern District Army was on its way to put down the rebellion. He pleaded to have just ten minutes on the air to explain to the public what he was trying to accomplish, but he was denied. To make matters worse, Haga found out that the Eastern District Army had not supported Hatanaka's plans, and he ordered him to leave the premises.

Hatanaka attempted to break into the recording studio to give himself airtime, but it was to no avail. He left the palace grounds and threw leaflets that explained his actions onto the streets, as he could not find any other avenue to explain his motives for the rebellion. An hour before the emperor broadcasted Japan's surrender, Hatanaka shot himself.

Japan officially surrendered on August 14th, 1945. General Douglas MacArthur presided over the proceedings on September 2nd, where they signed the Japanese Instrument of Surrender.

Occupied Japan

Between 1947 and 1952, the United States occupied Japan. The goals during that period were reform and recovery, with the ultimate goal being to design a treaty and peace agreement. Shigeru Yoshida served as prime minister and can be credited as one of the people who propelled Japan from a devastated country toward one with a healthy economy that matched pre-war levels.

First of all, a more democratic set of laws was deemed necessary, one that didn't favor elites or the wealthy. The power of the *zaibatsu* was immense to the point that it virtually controlled the economy, and greater pluralism was necessary in order to give people upward mobility. The emperor's role was nearly godlike to the point that any error he might make would reverberate throughout all of society and could have unintended effects. The intention of the US occupation was to grant Japan its freedom to initiate its own tenants and grant everyone the right to participate in creating laws that would work for them.

Because the country had incurred the negative effects of having itself managed by a class of elites, the imperial house, or wealthy businessmen, there was a need to remove senior leaders who would simply repeat the mistakes of the past. A new generation of leaders was essential in order to preserve freedom. It was also felt that the military shouldn't hold political positions.

Besides establishing the basis for democracy, the economy was utmost in terms of the survival and integrity of Japan as a sovereign country. Joseph Dodge, a banker from Detroit, acted as a consultant in reconstituting the financial system and balancing the budget. He also established an exchange rate for the Japanese yen.

Constitution of 1947

The post-war constitution, which replaced the Meiji Constitution, provided for a parliamentary government with members of the Diet being elected. It guaranteed the Japanese their rights of life, liberty, equality, academic freedom, and collective bargaining. The Diet was the sole legislative division, and the judicial branch was made independent.

Treaty of San Francisco

On September 8th, 1951, this treaty was signed between the Allied Powers and Japan. It established peaceful relations with Japan and stated a willingness to accept the judgment of the International Military Tribunal regarding war crimes committed during the war, including compensation for civilians and others who had suffered because of them. Japan was to have rights to its main islands but had to renounce all rights and titles to the Pescadores Islands, Taiwan, and the islands which it had gained during World War II. Japan retained some residual rights to the Ryukyu Islands, pending future revisions. By virtue of the 1971 Okinawa Reversion Agreement, the Ryukyu Islands were returned to Japan in 1972 and became one of the Japanese prefectures.

Full sovereignty was returned to Japan, but its military was dismantled and the country disarmed. Later, in 1954, the military was reorganized into a defensive force called the Japan Self-Defense Forces. Currently, that has changed with regard to participation in conflicts outside Japan that have an impact on Japanese security.

The Treaty of Mutual Cooperation and Security between the United States and Japan was created in 1951 and revised in 1952. It delineated mutual defense obligations and economic cooperation.

After the treaty was signed, the US continued to occupy Japan, and the Supreme Council of Allied Powers (SCAP) took on the task of rebuilding Japan and initiated efforts to revive its economy. Changes were instituted such as land reform, limitations placed on the power of the *zaibatsu*, reduction of the emperor's status in favor of the parliamentary system, granting women greater rights, renouncing its right to wage war by transforming it to serve a defensive function only, initiating tax reforms, and reducing inflation.

Inflation happened because Japanese industries were subject to the jolt of a sudden influx of contracts due to the international need for provisions for wars being fought abroad. Dodge had initiated an austerity program with price controls to help Japan prevent further inflation. SCAP, through his guidance, set up policies for Japan to avoid frequent governmental bailouts of failing companies since that would drain the national budget. In sectors like farming that were subject to intermittent losses, he recommended a system of controlled subsidies.

Korea

In 1910, Japan had annexed Korea, but after the war, the territory no longer belonged to them. Instead of placing the territory into the hands of one country, Korea was divided along the 38th parallel, with the northern portion going to the Soviet Union and the southern portion going to the United States. Although there were some attempts to unite the country after this initial division, by 1948, it was clear that it was not going to happen. North Korea, under the guidance of the Soviet Union, became communist in nature, leading some of the citizens to flee to South Korea, whose head of government was staunchly against communism. In 1950, North Korea attacked South Korea in the hopes of unifying both countries under one banner.

The war between North Korea and the United Nations forces, which were led by the United States, ended in 1953, with the war ending in a stalemate. The outcome is as yet unresolved, although discussions are currently underway to officially end the frozen conflict. The equipment needed by the United States, who fought heavily in the war, was provided by the Japanese "Model J" corporation, which is a corporation whose employees are trained specifically for their jobs. This sudden infusion of money was a boon to Japan, providing twelve billion dollars to its economy.

Chapter 11 –Heisei Era

In 1989, Hirohito died and was succeeded by his son, Akihito. When Akihito dies, he will be renamed as Emperor Heisei, meaning "achieving peace." The Heisei period spanned from 1989 to 2019.

Economy

After the rate of growth had exploded toward the end of Hirohito's term, it created what is called a "bubble economy." Bubbles predictably break, so lending institutions were in need of rescue from the national treasury. Predictably, the economy stagnated, and the banks and financial institutions then scrambled to recover their losses. As a stop-gap measure, low-interest loans were provided along with special tax-reduction incentives for lenders. This was unwise, as it became inevitable that weak borrowers were likely to default. This economic trauma forced Japan to turn from a "creditor nation" to a "debtor nation."

Some financial bodies sprung up because they assumed they could continue to be supported by the government because they were "too big to fail." The government, however, began to realize that this practice shouldn't continue, as it forced companies to provide loans at ridiculously low-interest rates and would force them to lower wages. Eventually, that reduced the money in circulation. Money was being hoarded in the hands of the very few who were "cash-rich," giving them nearly exclusive control. That, in turn, discouraged corporate investment, depleted the gross domestic product (GDP), and affected the stock market. From 1993 to 1996, there was a period of economic stagnation, and the cycle repeated again from 2009 to 2012.

Economic Planning

While Japan supports free enterprise, Japan isn't purely capitalist or socialist. For example, farmers receive subsidies, and the government often rushes in with monetary aid if any areas of the economy seem to be lagging behind others.

In terms of the labor market, only a very small segment of society was involved in the primary industries—mining, farming, and fishing. One-third of the population was in the industry sector, and a huge segment of society was engaged in the service sector. To prevent a segment of the population from sinking into absolute poverty, Japan felt that it had to monitor and control the economy to some extent. This function operates independently and is attached to the office of the minister of state. He, in turn, reports to the prime minister.

In 2001, an agency called the Ministry of Economy, Trade and Industry (METI) was established, consisting of multiple bureaus: 1) the Economic and Industrial Policy Bureau, 2) the Trade Policy Bureau, 3) the Trade and Economic Cooperation Bureau, 4) the Industrial Science and Technology Bureau and Environment Bureau, 5) the Manufacturing Industries Bureau, 6) the Commerce and Information Policy Bureau, as well as some other related agencies.

Environmental Planning

Because Japan is so dependent upon imports, a new ministry called the Environmental Management Bureau was created by reorganizing the 1971 Environmental Agency into a Cabinet-level ministry. In

2001, this was done by establishing a sub-Cabinet level called the Environmental Agency to reduce reliance on foreign sources through energy reduction. Japan looked toward creating a system of sustainable development. It was, in part, a reaction to the 1973 oil crisis that negatively affected Japan, as well as the rest of the world. Japan made an aggressive effort to build nuclear power plants and reduce electrical consumption. The other motivation for this had to do with safety protocols related to natural disasters such as earthquakes and tsunamis.

Art and Entertainment

Historically, during times of economic trauma, the entertainment industry tends to expand. When people become more stressful, companies take full advantage of that opportunity by providing a means of escape. The proliferation of art stimulated the industries that produced movies, video processes, TV, comics, and other media. The Japanese are well known for two very unique styles—anime and manga.

Anime, a particular animation style with a clearly recognizable character style, first appeared in 1917 but took root in Japan and across the world through the Heisei era. Large eyes with exaggerated emotions set in a disproportionately large head are characteristic of anime. In the beginning, this animated form consisted of a static background and figures on these backgrounds that were animated. The characters were drawn in ink, as the handier celluloid version required acetate that had to be imported from abroad. Once digital art was introduced, the celluloid animation cells were no longer necessary. Animation studios proliferated when Japanese artists were snapped up by the industry in many different countries. The subject matter was initially aimed at juveniles, but there arose a whole field of anime that appealed only to adults.

Manga refers to graphic novels and comic art using the Japanese language. Manga is said to have first been seen in scrolls dating back to the 12th century. Its character style was refined in the 19th century, and Oten Shimokawa developed it even further in 1917. During the Heisei era, it burgeoned into a multi-billion-dollar industry. The technique that was used was actually a reincarnation of a style created in the 19th century. Themes cover all the traditional fields, including action, horror, science fiction, mystery, history, and even adult pornographic content. Manga fired up the publishing industry as most of the material is in print.

Japan is very oriented toward preserving its historical roots, and manga presented a means by which Japanese history could be taught to the population. Eventually, this spread worldwide and provided Japan with an opportunity to become prominent on the international stage. The introduction of digital media created new markets for the spread of manga, and if a manga series is incredibly popular today, it is likely it will be made into a television series or movie.

The Role of Natural Disasters

Disturbances along geological fault lines in Japan have great significance because they are relatively frequent and affect the stability of the country. Japan lies on a fault line where two tectonic plates—the Pacific Plate and the Philippine Sea Plate—meet. As magma, the liquid core of the inner earth, moves, the upper solid layers, the earth's crust, shift. This movement results in widespread destruction of buildings and hundreds to thousands of innocent lives.

In 1995, an earthquake struck Kobe, which is located southwest of Tokyo. This earthquake reached 6.8 on the moment magnitude scale. Nearly 6,000 people died, and more than 400,000 buildings were severely damaged. The older buildings that had heavy roofs built to withstand typhoons collapsed from the top floor down in what is called a "pancake collapse." The port at Kobe was one of the largest container ports in the world, and this earthquake had disastrous effects worldwide, as thousands of international products were stored there, pending shipment. The Japanese economy had plateaued at this time, and the earthquake aggravated it. The stock market (the Nikkei Index) plunged, and Prime Minister Keizo

Obuchi was criticized for not having effective measures in place to protect Japan.

There had been several building codes adopted throughout the years, beginning in 1950. This code, called *kyu-taishin*, was a revision of the old 1924 code developed after the Great Kanto earthquake in 1923. It called for a reinforcement of the walls in order to hold up the roofs and would have eliminated the "pancake collapses" that occurred; however, the 1950 standards weren't enforced. The older buildings in Kobe, which had the heavy roofs, would never have collapsed if the 1950 standards had been applied. The *kyu-taishin* was replaced with the *shin-taishin* in 1981. This was designed to protect buildings from major damage resulting from mid-size quakes. In 2000, the new code required that buildings needed to pass inspection for foundation stability.

In 2004, the Chuetsu earthquake in Honshu, the largest island of Japan, occurred. Partially due to the cooperation of real estate developers in adhering to the *shin-taishin* amendment of the building code, only 68 people died.

In 2011, the Tohoku earthquake struck off the coast of Tohoku in the Iwate Prefecture, which lies 232 miles north of Tokyo. It spread to the northern island of Honshu because it had a 300-mile-long rupture line along the Pacific Plate. This is the most powerful earthquake ever recorded in Japan and the fourth in the world since people began recording earthquakes, reaching a magnitude of 9.0 to 9.1 and shifting the earth's axis by ten inches. Over 10,000 people died as a result of this and the tsunami that followed.

The tsunami flooded part of Honshu's eastern coast, although the area arose again several years later, and a partial nuclear meltdown occurred because it impacted the Fukushima Daiichi Nuclear Power Plant, disabling its emergency generators. This triggered a deliberate release of hydrogen gas so as to prevent a far worse after-event. Some of the ocean waters were also contaminated, and they had to build a sea wall to contain the contamination in 2013 because contamination was still leaking into the water. In order to curb rumors and misunderstandings, the Environmental Management Bureau introduced a public education program aimed at releasing accurate information about the occurrence.

Population Problems

In 2005, the population of Japan started to decline and continues to do so. Hence, the number of foreigners working in the country has increased in order to keep the economy flowing. Between 2007 and 2019, the number of foreign workers has quadrupled. Birth rates declined due to urbanization, the higher costs of raising children, and the rise of the nuclear family. In addition, there is a movement toward what is termed "herbivore men," which refers to men who aren't interested in marriage and don't spend a lot of time pursuing romantic relationships. The herbivore phenomenon is unrelated to vegetarianism or homosexuality and is more comparable to men who are intensely interested in pursuing a career and don't want to juggle it with marriage.

The Emperor Passes the Torch

In 2019, Emperor Akihito abdicated due to his old age and declining health. He served as a spokesman for environmental protection and human rights, and he made a lot of imperial visits to areas in the Pacific that had been intensely involved in World War II, like Okinawa and the Philippines. During his term, he became very focused on transnational issues. The Heisei era was a peaceable era, but commentators have issued the warning that too much pacifism could harm the future of the country because there have been threats and attacks made to first-world nations, of which Japan is one. There is an old Chinese proverb that asks: "Is it better to be a warrior in a garden or to be a gardener in a war?" That might well be applied to the next future era.

Akihito, who is now known as emperor emeritus, was succeeded by his son, Naruhito, in May of 2019. This initiated the Reiwa era, with Reiwa meaning "beautiful harmony."

Conclusion

Japan is about the same size as the US state of California and has a population of about 130 million people. For a country of modest size, it has one of the richest and most varied histories in the world. Like many other countries, it has run the gamut from primitive warring clans to a sophisticated and advanced culture. In the beginning, it was very much the product of one person whose family would control the country until another family came to take their place. Today, it has democratic institutions and promotes independent thought.

The Tokugawa shogunate was one of the most successful and prosperous administrations during a time when other countries were divided piecemeal among the power brokers of the day. Although isolation was its national policy during the 17th century, it created a unified national identity that other countries couldn't rival. This national identity helped Japan be very successful at the beginning of World War II, and although they ultimately lost the war, the following constitution and policies helped to create less of a gap between social classes, bringing the vast majority of the Japanese closer together.

The art and culture of Japan tie these people together even more and plays a prominent role in many other cultures around the world. Although they have been updated, art forms that were created in the 8th century still exist today. Japan is truly a wondrous place where modern thinking comfortably dwells with the ancient, creating a harmonious blend of ideas.

Here are some other books by Captivating History that we think you would find interesting

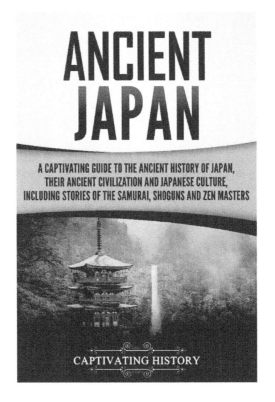

References

Adiss, S., Groemer, G and Rimer, J. (2006) *Traditional Japanese Arts and Culture: An Illustrated Sourcebook,* Harvard University Press.

Buell, R. (1922) *The Washington Conference.* Columbia University Press.

Chikamatsu. K. "Edo's Transportation Network," Retrieved from https://web-japan.org/tokyo/know/trans/tra.html.

Costello, J. (1981) *The Pacific War.* Columbia University Press.

Farris, W. (1996) *Heavenly Warriors: The Evolution of Japan's Military: 500-1300.* Harvard University Press.

"The First Sino-Japanese War," Retrieved from https://www.thoughtco.com/frst-sino-japanese-war-1894-95-1894-95-195784.

Harries, M. and Susie (2001) *Soldiers of the Sun.* Random House.

Hibbett, H. (2001) *The Floating World in Japanese Fiction,* Tuttle Publishing.

"In the Realm of Hungry Ghosts," Retrieved from https://www.goodreads.com/book/show/617702.In_the_Realm_of_H ungry_Ghosts.

Jansen, J. (2002) *The Making of Modern Japan.* Harvard University Press.

"Japanese Law Research Guide: Legal System & Statistics," Retrieved from https://libguides.uchastings.edu/japan-law/legal-system-stats.

Irokawa, D. (1985) *The Culture of the Meiji Period.* Princeton University Press.

Meyer, M. (1993) *Japan: A Concise History, 3rd ed.* Littlefield Adams.

Ravina, M. (2011) *The Last Samurai: The Life and Battles of Saigo Takamori.* John Wiley and Sons.

Saskisaka, M. "Economic Planning in Japan," Retrieved from https://onlinelibrary.wiley.com/doi/pdf/10.1111/j.1746-1049.1963.tb00638.x.

Suzuki, D. *Zen and Japanese Culture.* New York University PreWatanabe, T. (1984) "The Western Image of Japanese Art in the Late Edo Period," In Modern Asian Studies, Cambridge University Press.

Made in the USA
Monee, IL
22 December 2024

75194615R00080